AIR CAMPAIGN

TOKYO 1944–45

The destruction of Imperial Japan's capital

MARK LARDAS | ILLUSTRATED BY EDOUARD A. GROULT

OSPREY PUBLISHING
Bloomsbury Publishing Plc
Kemp House, Chawley Park, Cumnor Hill, Oxford OX2 9PH, UK
29 Earlsfort Terrace, Dublin 2, Ireland
1385 Broadway, 5th Floor, New York, NY 10018, USA
E-mail: info@ospreypublishing.com
www.ospreypublishing.com

OSPREY is a trademark of Osprey Publishing Ltd

First published in Great Britain in 2024

A catalog record for this book is available from the British Library.

ISBN PB 9781472860354; eBook 9781472860361;
ePDF 9781472860347; XML 9781472860330

24 25 26 27 28 10 9 8 7 6 5 4 3 2 1

Maps by www.bounford.com
Diagrams by Adam Tooby
3D BEVs by Paul Kime
Index by Fionbar Lyons
Typeset by PDQ Digital Media Solutions, Bungay, UK
Printed and bound in India by Replika Press Private Ltd.

Osprey Publishing supports the Woodland Trust, the UK's leading woodland
conservation charity.

To find out more about our authors and books visit www.ospreypublishing.com. Here
you will find extracts, author interviews, details of forthcoming events and the option to
sign up for our newsletter.

Author's note
The following abbreviations indicate the
sources of the illustrations used in this
volume:
AC – Author's Collection
LOC – Library of Congress,
    Washington, D.C.
NMAF – National Museum of the Air
    Force
PSAM – Palm Springs Air Museum
USAF – United States Army Air Force
USNHHC – United States Navy
    Heritage and History Command

Other abbreviations used within the text:
ECM – Electronic Countermeasure
IJA – Imperial Japanese Army
IJN – Imperial Japanese Navy

Author's dedication
To Nicholas Robbins. Thanks for the
opportunity to work for you on the
Lunar Gateway program.

CONTENTS

INTRODUCTION

Sixteen B-25s were spotted on the deck of the US Navy's aircraft carrier *Hornet* on Saturday morning, April 18, 1945. Their destination was Japan. The raid was conceived by US Navy Captain Francis S. "Frog" Low in January 1942.

Then Assistant Chief of Staff for antisubmarine warfare, Low had a thought completely unrelated to sinking German U-boats. US Army medium bombers launched from a US Navy carrier could attack Japan. The medium bombers' range, much greater than carrier aircraft, meant the Navy's invaluable carriers did not need to come suicidally close to Japan's coast to launch the strike. The bombers could not land on a carrier, but they could shuttle to Asian airfields in either the Soviet Union or the Republic of China, with which the United States was allied.

Three months later, the raid was about to become a reality. Raid planning had been transferred to Lieutenant Colonel James "Jimmy" Doolittle, then at Army Air Force headquarters in Washington, D.C. His first step was assigning himself to lead the raid. Negotiations to land at Vladivostok in Russian Siberia had fallen through. While allied with the United States against Germany and Italy, in 1942 the Soviet Union and Japan were at peace. The Soviets, fighting the Germans at the gates of Moscow, had no desire to be drawn into a war against Japan. Instead, the Mitchells would head to China.

The plan called for the bombers to launch at dusk on April 18, half an hour before sunset. They would fly over Japan at night, minimizing Japan's air defense threat. The task force carrying the B-25s was spotted by a Japanese picket boat just after sunrise that morning. It radioed a warning before being sunk. With the ships spotted, a decision was needed: scrub or press on with the attack?

Doolittle did not want to turn back. Doolittle, the task force commander, Vice-Admiral William Halsey, and *Hornet*'s captain, Captain Marc "Pete" Mitscher, agreed to push on. Instead of waiting until dusk, they would launch the aircraft immediately. Instead of launching 400nmi from Japan, they would take off 570nmi from their targets. At 0820hrs, the lead B-25, flown by Doolittle, lifted off *Hornet*'s deck. At roughly four-minute

A B-25 lifts off the deck of the aircraft carrier *Hornet* (CV-8) on its way to Tokyo. It was the first attack on the Japanese capital during World War II. In total, the raid consisted of 16 aircraft, 13 of which bombed the Tokyo urban area: Tokyo, Yokohama, and Yokosuka. (USNHHC)

intervals, 15 others followed. By 0919hrs, all were airborne, winging individually to Japan to save fuel.

Hornet, unable to operate its own aircraft with the B-25s on the flight deck, resumed naval carrier operations. Its sister carrier *Enterprise*, and the rest of the US Navy task force, headed away from Japan as Doolittle's raiders approached the enemy coast. The target for all but three B-25s was Tokyo. Ten would bomb targets in Tokyo proper. Three others aimed at Yokohama and Yokosuka on Tokyo Bay, within the Tokyo air defense region. Another three were flying to more remote targets; two to Nagoya and one to Kobe.

The crews flying the Mitchells expected to be slaughtered. They were attacking individually, in daylight rather than under cover of darkness. Most were attacking Tokyo, Imperial Japan's capital. They expected it to be heavily defended with both antiaircraft artillery and swarms of fighters. The Japanese were expecting them. Instead, all 13 B-25s sent Tokyo way experienced light opposition. Japanese civilians on the ground waved at the planes as they flew overhead. Some crews encountered fighters. Unless the B-25s shot first, the fighters ignored the Americans. (In some cases, the "fighters" were probably trainers.)

While the Japanese were prepared for an air raid, its timing was unexpected. Prior to the war's opening, defense officials assessed the ability of the US to strike Japan. They concluded an attack by long-range bombers was impossible in 1942. B-17s flying out of Clark Field in Luzon theoretically were within range of Tokyo, but by January 1942 Japan controlled most of the Philippines. The only way for Allied warplanes to reach Japan was by carrier. Their short range meant their carriers had to come within 300 miles of Japan's coast. Japan planned accordingly.

This included a line of picket boats 600 to 700nmi from Japan, one of which spotted the task force carrying Doolittle's aircraft at a distance twice that of carrier aircraft. Using simple arithmetic, the Japanese defense forces covering Tokyo expected a night attack or perhaps a carrier strike early the next morning. More accurately, the IJN expected an attack.

The raid was led by then-Lieutenant Colonel James "Jimmy" Doolittle, who is seen here tying Japanese medals to a bomb carried in the raid during a pre-mission ceremony and photo opportunity. The medals had been awarded to American officers, who contributed them to the Army, asking that they be returned to Japan in a suitable manner as soon as possible. (USNHHC)

The picket was an IJN vessel. It reported its find to the Navy, which failed to pass the word to the Army.

Two other coincidences reduced Japanese response. An air-raid drill was scheduled in Tokyo for April 18, announced the day before in Tokyo newspapers. It ran from 0900 to 1100hrs (ending an hour before the raiders arrived). Additionally, a military memorial ceremony was scheduled for the following Saturday, April 25. Army aircraft were practicing flyovers and Navy aircraft were conducting mock dogfights in the area. At noon, when Doolittle's aircraft arrived, there were only three Army fighters conducting air defense patrols over Tokyo. All 13 B-25s targeting Tokyo attacked successfully and escaped. All but one crashed trying to find their landing fields in China. (One was interned at Vladivostok.)

Each aircraft carried four bombs, either four 500lb high-explosive bombs or three 500lb bombs and an incendiary cluster. Each plane was given specific targets: an oil refinery, an iron foundry, a factory, a shipyard. All were directed to avoid hitting the Emperor's Palace, unmistakable in central Tokyo.

The damage inflicted – except to Japanese pride – was slight. A well-placed 500lb bomb was not enough to destroy even one factory. A single incendiary cluster had the potential to start serious fires, but the Tokyo Fire Department had turned out for the drill. Firefighting teams were still on alert an hour after the drill ended. They quenched any fires before they grew.

The most serious damage was to the submarine tender *Taigei* in Yokosuka. Renamed *Ryūhō*, it was completing conversion to a light aircraft carrier when one B-25 hit it with a 500lb bomb and several incendiaries. Instead of commissioning in May, repairs delayed its entry to service until November.

The damage to Japanese pride proved fatal. One result was a campaign to capture Midway in the Central Pacific and two islands in the US-held Aleutian archipelago (for which *Ryūhō* was unavailable). Japanese planners felt holding these would seal off any future carrier attacks on Japan. The US fleet (including *Hornet* and *Enterprise*) ambushed Japan's *Kidō Butai* off Midway, sinking four of Japan's six fleet carriers, crippling Japanese carrier aviation, and swinging the tide of the war from Japan to the Allies.

Such was the lure of Tokyo for both sides. In many ways, in World War II Tokyo *was* Japan. It was the national capital. In 1940, Japan's sprawling empire covered an eighth of the world, including possessions spread across the Pacific, half of Sakhalin Island, Formosa, Korea, Manchukuo, and large chunks of China. Its seat was in Tokyo, the world's third largest city and Japan's largest. The population of Tokyo proper, over 6.7 million in 1940, exceeded the combined population of Japan's next five largest cities.

But Tokyo went beyond the central city. It was part of a larger urban area that included adjacent Kawasaki (Japan's ninth largest city), with Yokohama (Japan's fifth largest city) butting up against Kawasaki. The three cities blended into one contiguous population center. A ring of suburbs surrounded this core, containing some of Tokyo's most important factories. They sprawled around both sides of Tokyo Bay and well into the Kantō Plain. The combined population of this municipal area was just under 10 million people.

It was also Japan's industrial, commercial, and cultural heart. Twenty-five percent of Japan's industrial workers lived in this urban complex. Kawasaki had Japan's largest concentration of industrial plants, almost all contributing to war production. Yokohama was Japan's most important seaport, accounting for one-quarter of the tonnage shipped in Japan's overseas trade. Tokyo and Kawasaki had extensive barge docks. It was Japan's most important railroad hub. Yokohama and Omiyo (17 miles north of Tokyo) were the most important railroad manufacturing, repair, and maintenance facilities in Japan. This area was also one of Japan's three most important aircraft manufacturing centers, with aircraft factories ringing the outskirts of Tokyo.

Over a score of airfields, both Army and Navy guarded Tokyo and its environs from attack. So did one of Japan's biggest naval bases, at Yokosuka. Army bases, barracks, and armories protected the area from invasion. Tokyo had the highest concentration of antiaircraft artillery in Japan. In World War II's game of military chess, Tokyo was Japan's queen. Remove it from the board, and Japan's war-making ability was crippled.

Jimmy Doolittle's visit was the first attack on Tokyo, but not the last. The urban complex received a 31-month respite after Doolittle's Raid, but for nearly a year, from November 1944 until three days after the war ended in August 1945, it would be the focus of a relentless air campaign to remove it from the playing field. During that time, the United States hurled nearly three dozen sets of air attacks on Tokyo and the surrounding defensive area. These involved more than the well-known B-29 missions. Carrier airstrikes and fighter sweeps also made important contributions. This is that story.

CHRONOLOGY

1941
December 7 Japan attacks Pearl Harbor, bringing the United States into World War II.

1942
April 16 Sixteen B-25s launched from the aircraft carrier *Hornet* for the first air raid on Tokyo.

1944
March Japan reorganizes its home air defense to defend against expected B-29 attacks.

June IJN defeats an attempt to create joint Army–Navy air defense of Japan.

June 15 Saipan invaded by United States forces.

July 21 Guam invaded by United States forces.

July 24 Tinian invaded by United States forces.

October 12 First B-29s arrive at Isley Field in Saipan.

November 1 One F-13A flies over Tokyo for the first time since Doolittle Raid. Conducts photoreconnaissance of Tokyo.

November 10 Harmon Field in Guam opens to B-29s.

November 24 First B-29 mission against Japan launched from the Marianas. Musashino aircraft engine plant near Tokyo bombed by 111 B-29s.

November 29–30 Twenty-nine Twentieth AF B-29s conduct a night raid against Tokyo's harbor area.

December 3 Daylight strike by B-29s against Musashino.

December 27 North Field in Tinian operational, B-29s arrive.

December 27 Daylight strike by B-29s against Nakajima aircraft plant and Musashino.

1945

January 313th Bombardment Wing begins combat operations.

January 9 Daylight strike by B-29s against Musashino.

January 19 Daylight strike by Twentieth AF B-29s against Kawasaki aircraft plant at Akashi.

January 21 Brigadier General Curtis LeMay relieves Haywood Hansell of command of the B-29s in the Marianas.

January 27 Seventy-six B-29s make high-level strike against Musashi.

February 10 Eighty-four B-29s fly over Tokyo area to bomb Nakajima aircraft factory at Ota.

February 15–17 Task Force 38 launches airstrikes against Tokyo and the surrounding area.

February 19 US Marines invade Iwo Jima.

February 19 Daylight strike by B-29s against clouded-over Musashino. One hundred and nineteen B-29s bomb Tokyo port area, 12 hit targets of last resort.

February 25 314th Bombardment Wing begins combat operations.

February 25 One hundred and seventy-two B-29s (the first three-wing strike) attack urban areas of Tokyo.

February 27 Daylight strike by Twentieth AF B-29s against Musashino.

March 9–10 First incendiary Toyko raid. Over 267,000 buildings destroyed; over 83,000 killed.

March 16 Central Field on Iwo Jima becomes operational.

April 1 Okinawa invaded by United States forces.

April 2 One hundred and twenty-one B-29s attack Nakajima factory in Tokyo.

April 3 Sixty-eight B-29s sent to clouded-over Nakajima aircraft factory at Koizumi and bomb targets of opportunity over Tokyo.

April 6 Kadena Airfield on Okinawa opens as an emergency landing field for B-29s.

April 7 First fighter escort for a B-29 mission, as P-51 escort a daylight mission to bomb the Nakajima aircraft factory at Tokyo. B-29 jamming of Japanese fire-control radars employed for the first time.

A B-29 from the 73rd Bombardment Wing flies over the Tokyo Prefecture early in the fight for Tokyo. The 73rd Wing fought in this campaign from November 1944 through August 1945. Since this was a daylight mission, the target for the day was most probably Nakajima's Musashi aircraft engine factory. (NMAF)

April 12 One hundred and five B-29s, escorted by P-51, bomb Nakajima aircraft factory and Shizuoka aircraft engine plant in Tokyo.

April 13–14 Second Tokyo incendiary attack, 330 B-29s sent on night raid.

April 15–16 Third Tokyo incendiary attack, 330 B-29s sent on night raid.

April 24 Daylight raid on aircraft and aircraft engine factories in Tachikawa, 101 B-29s sent.

May 5 58th Bombardment Wing operational in Marianas.

May 5–6 B-29s mine Tokyo Bay and maritime approaches to Tokyo, closing Tokyo, Kawasaki, and Yokohama to sea traffic.

May 23–24 Fourth Tokyo incendiary raid; 562 B-29s attack.

May 25–26 Fifth Tokyo incendiary raid; 464 B-29s attack.

May 29–30 Daylight incendiary raid on Yokohama; 454 B-29s sent.

June 10 Twenty-nine B-29s bomb Imperial Air Arsenal at Tachikawa.

June 26 315th Bombardment Wing conducts first combat mission.

July 4 P-51 Mustangs launch fighter sweeps against airfields in and around Tokyo. Between July 5 and August 6, they launch five more fighter sweeps against targets in Tokyo.

July 10–11 US Navy carrier aircraft attack airfields around Tokyo.

July 12 Fifty-three 315th Wing B-29s bomb Kawasaki Petroleum Facility.

July 17 US Navy carrier aircraft attack targets around Tokyo.

July 26 Eighty-three 315th Wing B-29s bomb Mitsubishi Oil Company and Hayama Petroleum.

August 1 Most B-29s sent on combat missions against Japan in a single day. Of 836 B-29s launched, 784 hit targets in Japan.

August 2 One hundred and twenty 315th Wing B-29s bomb Kawasaki Petroleum Facility, Mitsubishi Oil Company, and Hayama Petroleum.

August 6 *Enola Gay* drops an atomic bomb on Hiroshima.

August 8 The Soviet Union declares war on Japan.

August 8 B-29s bomb arsenal complex and aircraft factory in Tokyo.

August 9 *Bockscar* drops an atomic bomb on Nagasaki.

August 13–15 Task Force 38 launches carrier strikes against Tokyo.

August 15 Japan surrenders.

An aerial photograph capturing northern Tokyo prior to the March 9–10 fire raid. It was probably taken to assess bomb damage following the February 25, 1945 attack on Tokyo. The Imperial Palace compound can be seen center right. Pilots were under strict orders to avoid hitting the palace. (LOC)

ATTACKER'S CAPABILITIES
America's growing reach

The high-flying B-29s required hard-surfaced runways at least 6,000ft long. Engineers built six airfields capable of operating B-29s by expanding existing airfields in the Marianas and carving new ones out of jungle on Saipan, Guam, and Tinian. The first airfields were available only four months after their capture, a remarkable construction effort. (NMAF)

Attacking Tokyo, the capital of Imperial Japan, was high on the US wish list from December 1941 on. In April 1942, two highly valuable US Navy aircraft carriers were risked to strike Tokyo. That raid was encouraged by Franklin Roosevelt, President of the United States.

Yet the Doolittle Raid was unrepeatable. Tokyo lay at the very heart of Japan's Empire. As 1942 began, the nearest US-held territory to Tokyo was over 2,500 miles away. Not until July 1944, with the US capture of the first of the Marianas Islands, did the United States possess territory within bomber range of Tokyo. Even then, only one bomber, the largely untested B-29 Superfortress, could reach Japan. Not until February 1945 did the US hold bases within fighter range of Tokyo. Only one Army Air Force fighter, the P-51 Mustang, had the range to reach Tokyo.

Their numbers grew inexorably. In November 1944, a maximum effort strike on Tokyo consisted of 80 B-29s. By war's end, the United States could muster nearly 500 B-29s and several hundred P-51s. So did the airfields required to launch and maintain these aircraft. The US built the needed infrastructure mere months after taking the islands which held these airfields.

As for follow-up carrier attacks, not until November 1944 did the US hold ports close enough to Japan for further raids on Tokyo, and not until January 1945 did the US Navy feel confident enough to plan attacks on Tokyo. The Navy's carrier presence in the Pacific had grown from four fast carriers to 16, which could send up to 1,000 aircraft against a target.

This air armada was kept aloft by an unprecedented logistical train. Fuel, ammunition, food, and supplies required for the Army Air Force and US Navy to strike Tokyo crossed the Pacific from the North American coast to reach the Marianas Islands from which the B-29s operated, the Bonin Islands that housed the P-51s, and Ulithi Atoll from which the US Navy sortied. The effort was monumental. A single B-29 strike required over 1,000 tons of bombs.

The ability to target Tokyo was possible only because the United States possessed the right aircraft, infrastructure, weapons, and logistics capabilities. Moreover, they possessed each in numbers sufficient to overcome the inherent difficulties posed by using aerial bombardment to reduce a target, despite the distances that had to be traveled.

Aircraft

The United States used three types of aircraft to attack Tokyo: multi-engine land-based bombers, single-engine land-based fighters, and single-engine carrier aircraft. Only two multi-engine bomber types attacked Tokyo, the twin-engine B-25 medium bomber and the very heavy four-engine B-29 bomber. A third, the B-32, was used for photoreconnaissance in the last month of the war. The P-51 Mustang was the only land-based fighter used against Tokyo. Two carrier-based fighters, the F6F Hellcat and the F4U Corsair, and the SB2U Helldiver dive bomber and TBF/TBM Avenger torpedo bomber also participated in attacking Tokyo.

The B-25 was used for only one mission against Tokyo, the Doolittle Raid. It was selected because it was the only Army Air Force medium bomber capable of carrying 2,000lb of bombs 2,400nmi that could be launched from an aircraft carrier. While it went on to achieve a remarkable record during the rest of World War II, especially after being modified into a strafing aircraft, it never returned to Tokyo after April 1942.

The heavyweight in the campaign, literally and figuratively, was the Boeing B-29 Superfortress. It was the largest aircraft in the campaign, and delivered the greatest bombload. The May 25, 1945 B-29 incendiary raid against Tokyo released more bomb tonnage than all the US Navy airstrikes on Tokyo from 1942 through 1945 combined.

It was an extraordinary aircraft, at the limits of aviation technology when the prototype first flew in September 1942. It was fast, with a top speed of 357mph and a cruising speed of 290mph. With a wingspan of 141ft and fuselage length of 99ft, it was the world's largest bomber in 1944. It could reach a 31,850ft altitude while carrying the crew in a pressurized fuselage. Its four Wright R-3350 Duplex-Cyclone twin-row radial engines generated 2,200hp each.

With an empty weight of 74,500lb, it could carry 60,500lb of fuel, bombs, crew, and ammunition and still take off. It could carry up to 22,000lb of bombs in two bomb bays. With 10,000lb of bombs aboard, it had an effective combat range of 3,200 miles, within the 3,150-mile round-trip from its Marianas bases to Tokyo. It carried 12 .50cal machine guns and one 20mm cannon in four remote-controlled turrets and a manned tail position. All four turrets could be commanded by any of its gunners.

It was a difficult aircraft to fly, especially fully loaded. Due to its advanced features, it had early career reliability issues. (Most were fixed by March 1945.) It had a magnesium alloy

313th Wing and 314th Wing B-29s at Tinian. The B-29 represented a quantum jump in warplane capability. It could carry a larger load a longer distance and at a higher speed than any other heavy bomber flying in 1945. It also contained cutting-edge electronics and gunnery computing systems. (NMAF)

crankcase which caught fire when overheated. More B-29s were lost to mechanical issues and pilot error (especially on take-off) than to enemy action. Regardless, by 1945, it had become a war-winning aircraft. These were operated exclusively by the Twentieth Air Force during this campaign.

The P-51 was the Army Air Force's best World War II fighter and the only one it used against Tokyo. It was accidental, an American design ordered for the British. Initially used by the Army Air Force as a dive bomber, it was transformed when its original Allison engine was replaced by a Packard engine, a licensed version of the Rolls-Royce Merlin. The marriage produced a fighter that combined long range, high speed, outstanding high-altitude performance, superlative reliability, and excellent maneuverability.

It had a top speed of 440mph, a 362mph cruising speed, and could reach a 41,500ft altitude. With long-range fuel tanks it had a range of 1,600 miles, enough to escort B-29s to Tokyo from airfields on Iwo Jima, 750 miles away. With six .50cal machine guns it could shoot down any Japanese fighter.

A single-seat fighter, the long missions tested its pilots. It was vulnerable to navigation error and bad weather. On several occasions, Mustangs disappeared after entering storm fronts while flying to Japan. To ease navigation, a B-29 was often assigned to lead P-51 formations. The arrival of the P-51 doomed Japanese efforts to repel the B-29 with their fighter aircraft. All P-51s sent against Tokyo belonged to the Seventh Air Force.

The US Navy aircraft had significantly shorter ranges than the B-29 and P-51. Since their airfields moved with them, they did not need long range. They also carried a smaller bombload. All four naval aircraft could carry 2,000lb of bombs and rockets, including the Hellcat and Corsair fighters. (Fighters could carry up to 4,000lb, but normally carried only 2,000lb.) By February 1945, fleet carriers were routinely carrying 105 aircraft, 75 of which were fighters. The other 30 were split between Avengers and Helldiver bombers. Typically, half a carrier group's fighters flew as fighter bombers on attack missions, reverting to a fighter role after dropping the bombs. Their greater flexibility was why so few dedicated bombers were carried.

The F6F Hellcat was the most cost-effective fighter of the war. Daytime variants had six .50cal machine guns. A radar-equipped night fighter version normally carried four .50cal

The P-51 Mustang was an unintended addition to the Army Air Force fighter inventory. It proved its best fighter of World War II. With unprecedented range for a single-engine fighter, it was capable of escorting B-29s to Tokyo from bases on Iwo Jima. It outgunned any single-engine Japanese fighter. (AC)

machine guns and two 20mm cannon. They could carry six 5in rockets. It had a maximum speed of 391mph, a cruising speed of 200mph, a service ceiling of 37,300ft, and a range of 1,500 miles.

The F4U Corsair was the Navy's best fighter aircraft of World War II. It, too, had six .50cal machine guns, and could carry eight 5in rockets. It had a top speed of 417mph, a cruise speed of 220mph, a service ceiling of 36,000ft, and a 1,000nmi range. Because of its long nose, it was difficult to land on carriers and was not widely used as a carrier aircraft until 1945. A powerful and rugged aircraft, it was deadly in the air.

The Grumman TBF was the Navy's main torpedo bomber. It could carry one 18in aerial

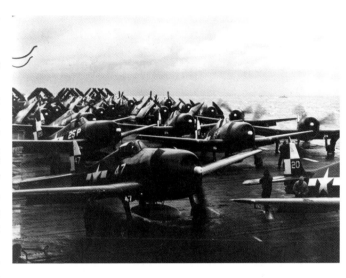

A deckload of F6F Hellcats await take-off from the flight deck of the aircraft carrier *Hornet*. (This is the second *Hornet*, CV-12, not CV-8, which carried the Doolittle B-25s.) An outstanding fighter, the F6F was the US's most cost-effective aircraft and could double as a bomber, and it was part of the US Navy's aviation punch. (USNHHC)

torpedo or up to 2,000lb of bombs internally. It had a crew of three. By 1945, it was armed defensively with two fixed, forward-firing .50cal machine guns, one .50cal in a power dorsal turret and one .30cal in a hand-held ventral mount. It had a top speed of 275mph, a cruising speed of 145mph, a service ceiling of 30,000ft, and a 1,000nmi range. The Navy's most versatile aircraft, it served as a torpedo bomber, daytime level bomber, antisubmarine warfare aircraft, and radar-equipped night bomber. General Motors built a licensed version called the TBM identical to the TBF.

The Curtis SB2C Helldiver carried 2,000lb of bombs internally, and an additional 500lb in underwing mounts. It had two fixed, forward-firing 20mm cannon and two flexible .30cal machine guns in a rear mount. It had a maximum speed of 295mph, a cruise speed of 158mph, a ceiling of 29,000ft, and a 1,165nmi range. It experienced structural and reliability problems throughout its career. Designed as a dive bomber, a role largely unneeded by 1945, it was used primarily for mast-top bombing or level bombing late in the war, a task performed better by fighter bombers. It was only carried on fleet carriers, and retained only against the hope an opportunity to use it against large warships might arise.

Facilities and infrastructure

The United States launched attacks on Tokyo from five major bases; airfields on Iwo Jima in the Bonin Islands, airfields on the Marianas Islands of Saipan, Tinian, and Guam, and the naval anchorage in Ulithi Atoll in the Caroline Islands. Saipan was captured in June 1944, Tinian in July, and Guam in August. Ulithi was taken in September 1944. Iwo Jima was invaded in February 1945 and secured in March. B-29s flew out of Saipan, Tinian, and Guam and used Iwo Jima as an emergency field. P-51s operated out of Iwo Jima. Fast carrier task groups launching airstrikes against Tokyo sortied from Ulithi.

All bases represented a revolution in force projection. Saipan, Guam, Tinian, and Iwo Jima had prewar airfields; none capable of operating B-29s. Two existing airfields at the Marianas, Saipan's Aslito Field (renamed Isley Field by the Americans) and Tinian's Gurguan Point Airfield (renamed West Field by the US) were massively expanded.

Four new B-29 airfields were carved out of the jungle: North Field at Ushi Point on Tinian, North Field near Pati Point on Guam, Northwest Field on the northwest corner of Guam, and Harmon Field on Guam. The last was a depot and aircraft maintenance base; the rest operational B-29 fields. All had crushed coral runways capable of allowing a fully loaded B-29 to take off. The Marianas also held other airfields used by fighters, transports,

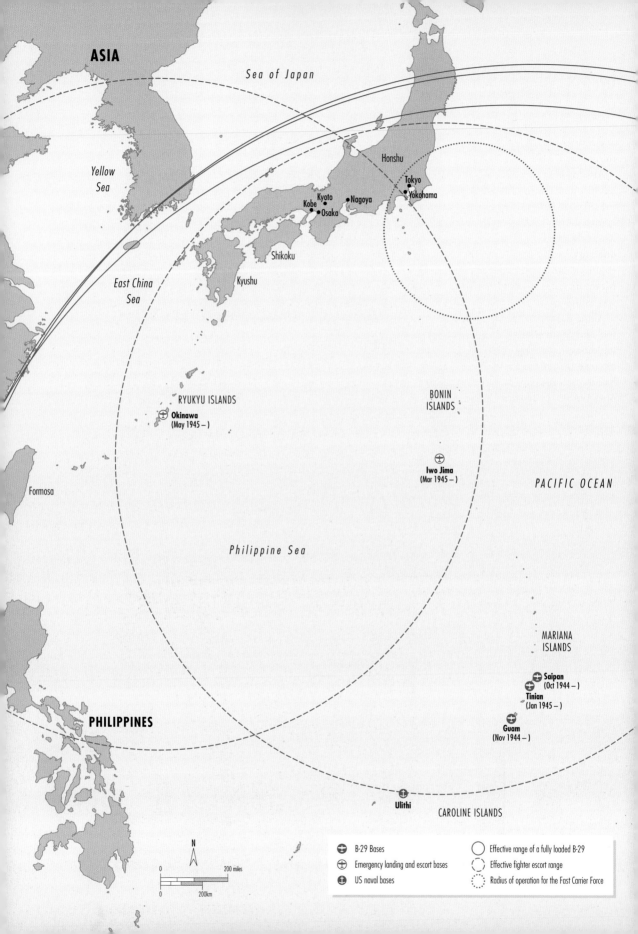

ASIA

Sea of Japan

*Yellow
Sea*

Honshu

● Tokyo
Kyoto ● Nagoya
Kobe ● Yokohama
● Osaka

*East China
Sea*

Shikoku

Kyushu

RYUKYU ISLANDS

⊕ **Okinawa**
(May 1945 –)

BONIN
ISLANDS

⊕ **Iwo Jima**
(Mar 1945 –)

PACIFIC OCEAN

Formosa

Philippine Sea

MARIANA
ISLANDS

⊕ **Saipan**
(Oct 1944 –)

⊕ **Tinian**
(Jan 1945 –)

⚓ **Guam**
(Nov 1944 –)

PHILIPPINES

⚓ **Ulithi**

CAROLINE ISLANDS

N

0   200 miles

0   200km

⊕ B-29 Bases

⊕ Emergency landing and escort bases

⚓ US naval bases

◯ Effective range of a fully loaded B-29

◌ Effective fighter escort range

⦿ Radius of operation for the Fast Carrier Force

OPPOSITE STRATEGIC OVERVIEW

and shorter-ranged bombers used by the Army Air Force, US Marine Corps, and US Navy to support US activities in the Marianas and protect the B-29s.

After Iwo Jima was taken, engineers transformed its three airfields (including the one left incomplete) into functioning air bases. Motoyama No. 1 (Airfield No. 1) was captured the first day of the US invasion, on February 19, and was quickly repaired. An aircraft first landed there on February 26. The first B-29 made an emergency landing on South Field (as it was renamed) on March 4, 1945. Motoyama No. 2 (Airfield No. 2) was extended into one capable of taking B-29s. After extending and broadening Runway 7 to 9,400ft x 200ft, engineers built a second parallel strip that was 9,800ft x 200ft. It became Center Field. Motoyama No. 3 (Airfield No. 3) was incomplete when captured. Named North Field, it was completed as a fighter strip and operational by April 24.

All of these airfields were simple landing strips that included revetments, hardstands, fuel and ordinance facilities, maintenance shops, and barracks, mess halls, and the other buildings needed to operate large numbers of aircraft. The typical time between the start of construction and completion was two months. Isley Field, captured June 16–17, 1944, had the first combat mission depart from it on October 28, 1944. Tinian's North Field was operational 45 days after capture.

The US Navy's Fast Carrier Force, Task Force 38 or 58 (the number depending on the admiral commanding it) provided a mobile base from which over 1,000 aircraft could operate. The naval anchorage at Ulithi, captured in September 1944, was a functional base a month later. It permitted the US Navy to operate off Japan's coast. (USNHHC)

All were far from Tokyo. Saipan was 1,460 miles, Tinian 1,470 miles, and Guam 1,570 miles. This was just barely within the B-29's 3,200-mile range. Iwo Jima was 750 miles, almost exactly halfway between the Marianas and Tokyo. Its capture deprived Japan of its last airfield capable of attacking the Marianas while giving B-29s a safe haven when too damaged to reach the Marianas.

Ulithi gave the US Navy a refuge within striking distance of Japan. Captured unopposed, by December 1944 it was the US Navy's largest naval base. It was only 1,320 miles (1,100nmi) from Tokyo. Its anchorage could hold the entire US Navy. It had been transformed into a major supply and repair base with floating drydocks, one of which could carry an Iowa-class battleship. Its repair facilities were manned with 6,000 ship fitters and other repair personnel. To supply the Navy operating out of it, it contained vessels to distill fresh water, bake fresh bread, and provide other comforts for ships and sailors.

Operating out of Ulithi was the Fast Carrier Force, either Task Force 38 or Task Force 58, depending on whether it was part of the Third Fleet or Fifth Fleet. (The ships of both fleets were the same. The only thing that changed was the fleet number.) Third Fleet was commanded by Admiral William "Bill" Halsey, Fifth Fleet by Admiral Raymond Spruance. The two admirals and their staff swapped command of the ships as one executed the current operation while the other planned the next one.

In February 1945, when the Navy launched its first Tokyo strikes, the Fast Carrier Force was made up of 11 fleet carriers and five light carriers, supported by eight fast battleships, five heavy cruisers, nine light cruisers, and 67 destroyers. The carriers provided air power. Their escorts protected the carriers from enemy aircraft, warships, and submarines. The Fast Carrier Force's slowest ship could steam 28 knots.

Nine fleet carriers belonged to the Essex class. These carriers displaced 35,000 tons loaded. Their waterline was 820ft long with an 862ft flight deck. They could reach 32.5 knots and cruise 20,000nmi at 15 knots. They had powerful antiaircraft batteries and excellent internal protection. Their air groups totaled 105 aircraft. The other two were the prewar *Saratoga* and *Enterprise*. Elderly and inferior to the Essex class, they were used for night carrier operations, with smaller, more specialized air groups.

Iwo Jima provided airfields from which P-51s could operate. It also offered a refuge where B-29s could land when they could not reach their Marianas bases due to battle damage or fuel shortages. *Flak Alley Sally* from the Sixth Bombardment Group refuels there in March 1945, shortly after the airfield opened. (NMAF)

There were five Independence-class light carriers. Each had a 600ft waterline and a 552ft flight deck. They displaced nearly 15,000 tons fully loaded and could reach a top speed of 31 knots. They could steam 13,000nmi at 15 knots. Designed to carry 45 aircraft, they typically carried 31 to 35. They were modified from Cleveland-class light cruisers to light carriers while under construction.

They were supported by a fleet train of oilers, ammunition ships, supply ships, and escort carriers. The oilers refueled the warships; the rest supplied everything from beans to spare aircraft. Doctrine was to resupply the Fast Carrier Force before it entered combat, with the fleet train withdrawing to safety while the attack was underway.

More remarkable than the existence of these bases and the Fast Carrier Force was the effort to keep the airfields, naval bases, aircraft, and ships supplied with fuel, food, and ammunition, and keep their crews fed, clothed, and housed. Everything, including the equipment and most of the materials to build the bases, had been shipped from North America's Pacific coast, 5,800 miles from the Marianas, 6,600 miles from the Bonin Islands, and 6,200 miles from Ulithi.

A single B-29 fully loaded and fueled for daytime Tokyo mission required 34,000lb of 100-octane aviation gasoline. It carried a quarter-ton of machine-gun and 20mm ammunition for its defensive guns and up to 8,000lb of bombs. (The night missions traded fuel and machine-gun ammunition for greater bombload.) A carrier deck strike (roughly 50 aircraft) consumed around 50 tons of munitions and 60 tons of fuel. By March 1945, the Army Air Force was routinely flying 300-bomber attacks against Tokyo, while the Navy was routinely launching 30 or more deck-strike attacks per day during intense combat operations.

Moving sufficient supplies – food, clothing, spare parts as well as munitions and fuel, became the limiting factor in the campaign. The US met that challenge. In some cases, it meant eliminating less efficient systems. B-24s could have operated from Iwo Jima and attacked Tokyo. However, a single B-29 could do the work of three B-24s. Given that, it made more sense not to add to the logistics burden by using B-24s.

The B-29 carried ten 0.50cal machine guns in four remote-controlled turrets. They could be fired by any of the gunners (including the tail gunner in a manned position) using an analog computer system. The gunners operated the guns from positions like this one, with the gunner in a dome atop the Superfortress. (NMAF)

Weapons and tactics

During World War II, the US Army and the US Navy used common weapons, especially for aircraft. Commonality was indicated by the designation "AN" for Army–Navy. Navy and Army Air Force aircraft shared the same guns, ammunition, and bombs. These included the AN/M2 Browning .50cal machine gun, the AN/M1919 .30cal machine gun, and the AN/M2 20mm cannon. All three were air-cooled, and mechanically reliable.

The M2 20mm cannon was a US-licensed version of the Hispano-Suiza HS.404 Mark II 20mm cannon. It was used on the Helldiver and B-29. With a muzzle velocity of 2,800fps, it fired a 4.6oz (130g) projectile, with a rate of fire of 700 to 750 rounds per minute. It had armor-piercing, high-explosive, and incendiary rounds. The high-explosive round charge was between 0.21 and 0.39oz (6 to 11g).

The AN/M2 .50cal fired a 52g bullet with a muzzle velocity of 2,910fps. It fired 750 to 850 rounds per minute. Rounds could penetrate 1in

OPPOSITE CONDUCTING A FIRE RAID

of armor; it was potent against ships, ground vehicles, and buildings as well as other aircraft. It was the standard US weapon of the campaign, carried on bombers and fighters.

The M1919 .30cal was lighter, firing an 11g round with a muzzle velocity of 2,800fps. Aircraft versions fired 1,200 to 1,500 rounds per minute. It was effective primarily against aircraft or troops in the open. It was used as a defensive gun on Navy bombers.

The US used a variety of bombs against Tokyo. Most commonly deployed were incendiary and general purpose high-explosive bombs, but specialized types, parafrag, armor-piercing bombs, torpedoes, and High Velocity Aircraft Rocket (HVAR), also saw use.

The incendiary bombs used were primarily the M-47, M-69, and M-74 incendiaries. The M-69 and M-74 were 8in long, with a diameter of 3in, and hexagonal cross-section steel pipes. Each weighed around 6lb, clustered in containers of 40 to 60 incendiaries which opened at 2,000ft. They were first used against Tokyo during the Doolittle Raid. The M-69 had a streamer to slow its descent and increase the scatter; the M-74 lacked the streamer, but had more incendiary material. The M-47 was a repurposed chemical-warfare bomb. Instead of filling them with poison gas, these thin-skinned bombs were filled with napalm and phosphorous, sometimes mixed.

The high-explosive general purpose bombs used were the 500lb AN-M64, the 1,000lb AN-M65, and the 2,000lb AN-M66. The weight was total weight of the bomb. They had a cast or machined casing filled with explosive. The AN-M64 held 262lb of explosive, the AN-M65 530lb, and the AN-M66 1,061lb. The rest of the weight was the metal casing. The 500lb bomb was excellent against unarmored ships, vehicles, and wood-frame or lightly constructed buildings. They proved ineffective against reinforced concrete structures. The 1,000lb bomb worked better against metal buildings and other built-up structures (or lightly armored ships), but against reinforced concrete structures (such as aircraft factories) 2,000lb bombs were needed.

The parafrag was a modified 500lb bomb, created by wrapping the bomb in steel wire, adding a parachute (to slow its fall), and sometimes adding a 3ft pipe with a fuse to the nose. This ensured the bomb exploded 3ft above the ground, sending shredded metal everywhere. It was deadly against aircraft on the ground and personnel in the open. The HVAR was a 5in rocket with a 45lb warhead. Both, carried by single-engine aircraft, were used for airfield suppression.

The B-29 could hold up to 20,000lb of bombs in two bomb bays, but normally carried between 5,000lb and 12,000lb on Tokyo missions. Here an armorer prepares a load of M-64 500lb general purpose bombs for a mission. The M-64 was the most commonly used general purpose bomb in this campaign. (NMAF)

Tactics depended on the mission. For bombing distinct targets, the Twentieth Air Force used high-level precision bombing. The aircraft attacked a target in a tight formation known as a battle box, at 30,000ft, using the Norden bombsight. Prewar testing showed it had a circular error probability of 75ft. Army Air Force doctrine maintained using the Noden bombsight while flying a tight formation over a target could destroy it in one mission.

Its performance proved problematic over Japan due to high winds, including the recently discovered and poorly understood jet stream. If the bomb run were made into the wind, the approach was suicidally slow. With the wind, they were too fast for accurate bombing. Crosswind approaches blew the bombs too far crosswind for the bombsight to adjust. Low clouds

Conducting a fire raid

The devastating fire raids of 1945 followed a tightly choreographed yet highly flexible sequence. The four steps to a fire raid are shown in this diagram.

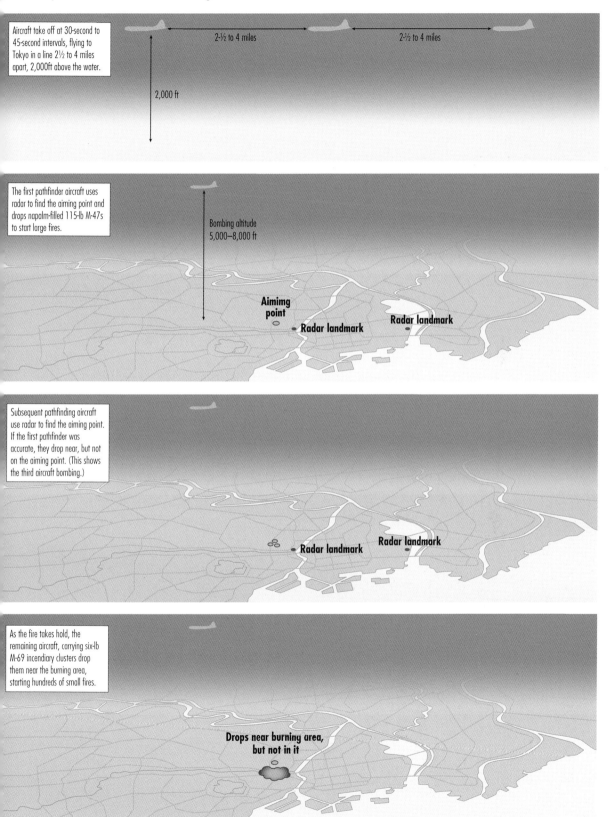

Aircraft take off at 30-second to 45-second intervals, flying to Tokyo in a line 2½ to 4 miles apart, 2,000ft above the water.

2-½ to 4 miles

2-½ to 4 miles

2,000 ft

The first pathfinder aircraft uses radar to find the aiming point and drops napalm-filled 115-lb M-47s to start large fires.

Bombing altitude 5,000–8,000 ft

Aimimg point

Radar landmark

Radar landmark

Subsequent pathfinding aircraft use radar to find the aiming point. If the first pathfinder was accurate, they drop near, but not on the aiming point. (This shows the third aircraft bombing.)

Radar landmark

Radar landmark

As the fire takes hold, the remaining aircraft, carrying six-lb M-69 incendiary clusters drop them near the burning area, starting hundreds of small fires.

Drops near burning area, but not in it

frequently obscured the target from the high-flying B-29s. Airborne radar technology, at least through June 1945, was too primitive to permit precision bombing of a factory. The alternative was to bomb at medium altitudes – 15,000 to 24,000ft – which was too dangerous for unescorted B-29s while Japan's day fighter force was intact.

The alternative was mass incendiary attacks at night. Bombers attacked under cover of darkness from low altitudes, 8,000 to 12,000ft. Japanese cities were vulnerable to fire, especially Tokyo. Highly built up, 40 percent of the most densely populated areas of Tokyo were covered by roofs. In residential areas of US towns, 10 percent was. Further Japanese buildings were largely wood and lathe, with small factories and machine shops intermixed with residences, occupied by those who worked there.

Night raids dispensed with formations. Aircraft flew individually to Tokyo, spaced 30 to 45 seconds apart (the take-off interval from each runway). The best-trained crews constituted the pathfinders, arriving first. They carried M-47s, which started "appliance fires," large enough to require sending out a fire engine in response. Each pathfinder carried 60 or more of these, scattering them over the target area. Pathfinders following the lead B-29 dropped their M-47 near, but not where the previous fires had been started. Within ten minutes, hundreds of appliance fires were burning, fully occupying Tokyo's fire department.

The main bomber force followed, carrying M-69s or M-74s. Each Superfortress dropped over 6,000 incendiaries, which scattered over an acre. As before, they dropped their bombs next to the burning area. A single 6lb incendiary could be doused by a bucket of sand, but so many were dropped, not all could be extinguished. The fires grew, merged, and burned out of control. The only escape was to flee, as the firefighting teams became overwhelmed.

Daytime bombing improved in April 1945, when Iwo Jima airfields permitted fighter escorts. Fighter escorts used new tactics designed for the B-29s' speed. The P-51s flew ahead of the bomber formation, to prevent head-on attacks. Japanese fighters attempting to penetrate the front of the formation were intercepted and shot down. They could only reach the bombers from the sides, which demanded highly skilled deflection shots, or astern, closing with their target at 50 to 100mph. That made them easy targets for B-29s' radar-laid defensive guns. Since the P-51s cruised at the same speed as the B-29s, this turned escort missions into fighter sweeps.

The US Navy's main focus during this campaign was land targets. It began a series of raids by first attacking enemy airfields. After a fighter sweep, the next step was to have bombers, generally Avengers, crater runways as shown here. The runways had to be repaired before flight operations resumed. (AC)

Although they did go after merchant shipping in Tokyo Bay and Japanese warships in Yokosuka Naval Base, US Navy aircraft primarily attacked land targets when they struck Tokyo: airfields, aircraft factories, and shore installations. The Navy typically began a day with a fighter sweep, to clear the sky of any enemy aircraft aloft and destroy any aircraft unwilling to fly on the ground. The fighters strafed antiaircraft positions near that day's targets. That left bombers and fighter bombers free to attack.

Bomb runs were typically made at medium to low altitudes: mast-top to as high as 5,000ft. At low altitudes, the small size and speed of the naval aircraft made them hard to hit. Low-level bombing was also highly accurate. Often, an airfield strike started with fighters and fighter bombers strafing the field, followed almost immediately by Avengers dropping parafrags. In July and August, Army Air Force P-51s imitated these tactics, conducting massive fighter sweeps over Japanese airfields. These strikes depended on strafing, as external fuel tanks were necessary to reach Tokyo from Iwo Jima.

DEFENDER'S CAPABILITIES
Guarding the Empire's heart

Tokyo's defense was complex and multi-layered. It involved a geographic area larger than the Tokyo–Kawasaki–Yokohama urban complex. It encompassed most of the southeastern half of the Kantō Plain. It required coordination of fighter aircraft, antiaircraft artillery, electronic intelligence (including radar), and civil defense.

While aircraft and antiaircraft artillery were part of the defense, they were not the most important elements. Being able to put aircraft and guns in position to intercept attacking aircraft was as important as their actual numbers. That required a robust system to track incoming attackers and to direct combat assets towards them. Radar and ground control sent aircraft where they were needed. Civil defense mitigated damage done by bombing. Only all elements working together could best protect Tokyo and its environs.

One constraint was Japanese military doctrine. This was felt in two ways. The first was resource allocation. Japan's military divided the country into sectors and assigned resources to these sectors, where they remained. Units could be reassigned, but even highly mobile resources, such as aircraft, remained within organizational boundaries.

Tokyo belonged to the Eastern District Army, the field army responsible for defense of the Kantō Plain. Only IJA units belonging to this command were used to defend Tokyo. Similar limitations constricted the availability of IJN forces. Only units assigned to or temporarily attached to the Yokosuka Naval District defended Tokyo. It was headquartered at Yokosuka Naval Base at the entrance to Tokyo Bay.

The task was muddled by rivalry between the IJA and the IJN. Both had assets – aircraft, antiaircraft artillery, and intelligence – valuable to Tokyo's defense. Although the Army was the senior service, neither service would subordinate its efforts to the other. The result was their efforts were uncoordinated, reducing the ability for Japan to defend its capital.

The other doctrinal issue complicating Tokyo's defense was the Japanese attitude to defense. Army and Navy emphasized attack over defense. They believed using resources for defense reduced offensive capability. This resulted in shortages of antiaircraft guns and interceptor aircraft. The money to procure them was felt better spent on field artillery and bombers.

The Kawasaki Ki-61 *Hien* was the fighter most associated with the defense of Tokyo. It saw combat for the first time during the Doolittle Raid, and was one of the mainstays against the B-29. Its armament was light for fighting B-29s, but superior to those of prewar fighters. Some were stripped down to allow them to ram B-29s. (AC)

The resources allocated to defense were focused on defensive weapons, not defensive systems. The defense of Tokyo against air attack required flexibility and proactive action. Tokyo was ill-prepared for an aerial siege.

Aircraft

Japan's biggest limitation with the aircraft defending Tokyo was numbers. There were never enough. Japan neglected fighters in favor of bombers. While Japan had between 2,000 and 2,500 combat-capable fighter aircraft available between October 1944 and August 1945, most were stationed overseas, opposing the Allied advance. There were only 370 to 385 fighters in the Home Islands (Hokkaido, Honshu, Shikoku, Kyushu, and the islands immediately around them) between October 1944 and March 1944. Their numbers jumped to 450 in April 1945, gradually increasing to 535 at war's end.

This did not mean 370 to 535 fighters were available to defend Tokyo. The Imperial Army and Navy parceled out aircraft geographically. The Eastern District Army, tasked with Tokyo's defense, had only the 90 fighters of the 10th Flying Division available. They could request the assistance of IJN's 302nd Air Group, which was part of the Yokosuka Naval District, consisting of another 30 to 50 aircraft. It was part of the 71st Air Flotilla, headquartered out of Yokosuka. Their primary responsibility was defense of Navy assets in and around Tokyo Bay.

Those fighters were manned by pilots inferior to those of their opponents. In December 1941, Imperial Army pilots received 500hrs and Imperial Navy pilots 700hrs of flight training before being sent to operational units. By October 1944, when the campaign against Tokyo began, this dropped to 150 and 300hrs respectively, less than half for each service. (By 1945, Army Air Force pilots received 300hrs of flight training and US Navy pilots 600hrs of flight training, with the Army pilots receiving additional flight time in backwaters before being committed into intense combat.)

Although a few early-war IJA and IJN veterans survived and were flying in late 1944, most were dead. Once assigned to a frontline unit, they remained in combat until dead or too badly wounded to continue. The injured, if they recovered, were assigned to new units, where they would typically remain. (The pace of the Pacific air war was such that in the months they took to recover, their old unit had typically been destroyed.) Most pilots defending Tokyo were late-war trainees, eager but inexperienced.

The Allies cut Japan's access to their Southeast Asian oilfields in January 1945. Thereafter, the Japanese aircraft were hobbled by fuel shortages. This affected training and operational flying, further reducing readiness. In April 1945, Imperial High Command opted to conserve aircraft, including fighters, to oppose a future invasion of the Home Islands. The result was aircraft became increasingly less relevant to Tokyo's defense as the campaign continued.

The aircraft defending Tokyo fell into two broad categories: daytime fighters and night fighters. The daytime fighters were all single-engine aircraft. The night fighters were a combination of radar-equipped twin-engine fighters and modified single-engine fighters. Typically, there were between 18 to 24 night fighters assigned to guard Tokyo; the rest were daylight aircraft.

Each service had its own aircraft of both types, even when that made no sense. It was understandable why the Imperial Navy needed fighters capable of carrier landings. But they also had built twin-engine fighters incapable of landing on aircraft carriers, and several of the late-war fighter designs the Imperial Navy ordered never operated from carriers. Army–Navy rivalry yielded duplication of effort, smaller production runs, and loss of economy of scale.

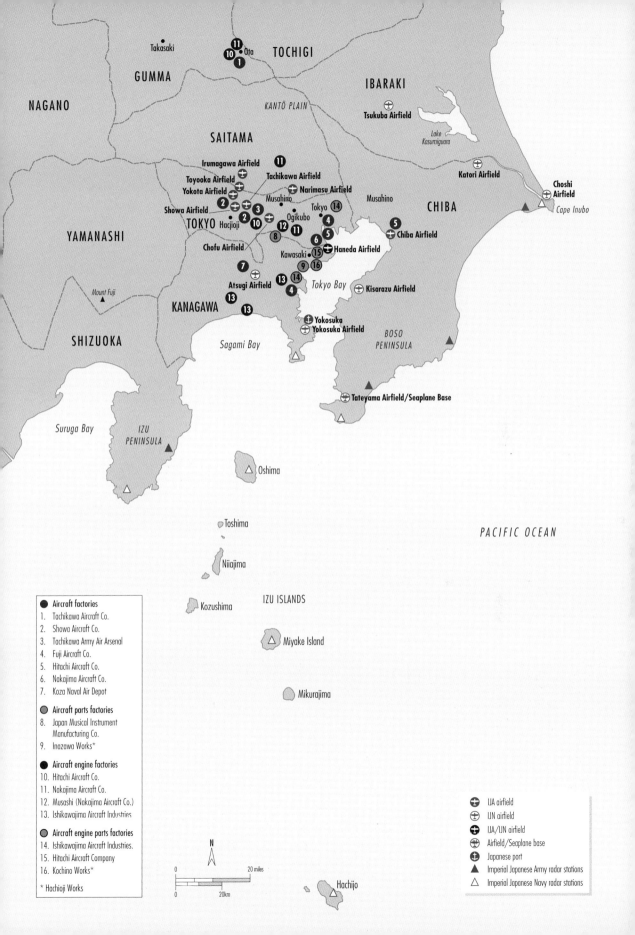

TAKASAKI • • Ōta
Takasaki

TOCHIGI

GUMMA

⑪
⑩ • Ōta
①

NAGANO

KANTŌ PLAIN

IBARAKI

⊕ Tsukuba Airfield

SAITAMA

Lake Kasumigaura

Irumagawa Airfield ⊕
⑪

Toyooka Airfield ⊕
Tachikawa Airfield

Yokota Airfield ⊕
⊕ Narimasu Airfield

Musashino

Katori Airfield ⊕

CHOSHI Airfield ⊕ ⊙
Cape Inubo

Showa Airfield ⊕
② ②

③
Musashino

TOKYO
Hachioji
② ⑩

Tokyo
⑭

Ogikubo ④

CHIBA

⑤
⊕ Chiba Airfield

YAMANASHI

⑫ ⑪
⑧
Chofu Airfield

⑥ ⑤

⑮ ⊕ Haneda Airfield
Kawasaki •

⑦
⑨
⑬ ⑭
⑯
④

Tokyo Bay

⊕ Kisarazu Airfield

Mount Fuji ▲

Atsugi Airfield ⊕

⑬
⑬

KANAGAWA

⊙ Yokosuka
⊕ Yokosuka Airfield

Sagami Bay

SHIZUOKA

Suruga Bay

BOSO PENINSULA ▲

△

⊕ Tateyama Airfield/Seaplane Base

IZU PENINSULA ▲

△ Oshima

PACIFIC OCEAN

⊙ Toshima

Niijima

IZU ISLANDS

△ Miyake Island

Kozushima

Mikurajima

● **Aircraft factories**
1. Tachikawa Aircraft Co.
2. Showa Aircraft Co.
3. Tachikawa Army Air Arsenal
4. Fuji Aircraft Co.
5. Hitachi Aircraft Co.
6. Nakajima Aircraft Co.
7. Koza Naval Air Depot

● **Aircraft parts factories**
8. Japan Musical Instrument Manufacturing Co.
9. Inazawa Works*

● **Aircraft engine factories**
10. Hitachi Aircraft Co.
11. Nakajima Aircraft Co.
12. Musashi (Nakajima Aircraft Co.)
13. Ishikawajima Aircraft Industries

● **Aircraft engine parts factories**
14. Ishikawajima Aircraft Industries.
15. Hitachi Aircraft Company
16. Kochino Works*

* Hachioji Works

N ↑

0 ————— 20 miles
0 ————— 20km

⊕ IJA airfield
⊕ IJN airfield
⊕ IJA/IJN airfield
⊕ Airfield/Seaplane base
⊙ Japanese port
▲ Imperial Japanese Army radar stations
△ Imperial Japanese Navy radar stations

△ Hachijo

The principal Imperial Army single-engine fighters defending Tokyo were the Nakajima Ki-43 *Hayabusa* (Peregrine Falcon – Allied code-name Oscar), Nakajima Ki-44 *Shoki* (Devil Queller – Allied code-name Tojo), Kawasaki Ki-61 *Hien* (Flying Swallow – Allied code-name Tony), and Nakajima Ki-84 *Hayate* (Gale – Allied code-name Frank). The Imperial Navy had the Mitsubishi A6M Zero (Allied code-name Zeke), Mitsubishi J2M *Raiden* (Thunderbolt – Allied code-name Jack), and Kawanishi N1K-J *Shiden* (Violet Lightning – Allied code-name George). The *Hayabusa* and Zero entered service before the Pacific War began. The *Shoki* was introduced in 1942; the other four first flew in 1943, entering combat in 1944.

All these aircraft had limitations reducing effectiveness. Early-war designs lacked armor or self-sealing gas tanks and were lightly built, for greater range and maneuverability. They were lightly armed by late-war standards, with only two to four guns or cannon. They were unlikely to knock down a B-29 or US Navy carrier aircraft on a single pass. All three early war fighters had top speeds below the B-29's top speed and were only marginally faster than the B-29's cruise speed. A single pass was all they were likely to get against a B-29 formation.

The Zero and *Hayabusa* delivered outstanding performance at low and medium altitudes, but were sluggish above 24,000ft. The *Shoki*, intended as a high-altitude bomber interceptor, was also sluggish above 30,000ft. They found it difficult to reach B-29s flying at 30,000 to 31,500ft, and were outclassed by late-war US Navy aircraft.

The Mitsubishi J2M-3 *Raiden*, code-named "Jack" by the Allies, was the Imperial Navy's best fighter. Its biggest weakness was its armament, two 12mm machine guns and two 20mm cannon. Light for attacking B-29s, it was only adequate against single-engine warplanes. This aircraft was captured and used for evaluation by the United States. (USNHHC)

The late-war *Hien*, *Hayate*, *Raiden*, and *Shiden* were significantly better aircraft. They had armor and self-sealing gasoline tanks. They could match the altitudes of the high-flying Superfortresses. The *Hien* had an inline V-12 powerplant generating 1,159hp. The rest had radial engines with a higher horsepower – 1,473 to 2,041hp at sea level. The *Hien* and *Raiden* had top speeds of 360 to 370mph; the *Hayate* and *Shiden* could top 400mph. Standard armament for the *Hien* was light: two 7.9mm machine guns and two 20mm cannon. The rest carried four 20mm cannon or two 20mm cannon and two 12.7mm machine guns, equivalent to the firepower of late-war Allied fighters.

The Zero and *Hayabusa* were the most widely available fighters, even in 1944–45. Over 11,000 Zeroes and nearly 6,000 *Hayabusa*s were built. *Hayate* production topped 3,400 aircraft. The *Shoki* had a run of 3,000 before production ceased early in 1945. Around 3,000 *Hien* were built, 1,500 *Shiden*, and under 700 *Raiden*.

Four night fighters existed, the twin-engine Army Kawasaki Ki-45 *Toryu* (Dragon Slayer – Allied code-name Nick), Kawasaki Ki-102 (Allied code-name Randy), and Navy Nakajima J1N1 *Gekkō* (Moonlight – Allied code-name Irving), and a night fighter version of the *Hayate*.

The *Toryu* and *Gekkō* were prewar long-range escorts; both proved unsatisfactory. They were large enough to carry the airborne radar sets Japan developed during the war and were converted to night fighters. Both had top speeds well below that of the B-29 and barely above its cruise speed. They also performed poorly at high altitude. The Ki-102 was the replacement for the *Toryu*. It was faster (360mph top speed) with a 32,000ft ceiling. Their utility as night fighters was reduced due to poor radar performance and poor training for the radar operators.

All were heavily armed, carrying a mix of 12.7mm machine guns and 20mm, 37mm, and 57mm cannon. In addition to forward-firing guns, the *Gekkō* and Ki-102 were equipped with a pair of upward-firing 20mm cannon. The night fighter version of the *Hayate* also carried upward-firing cannon. These allowed aircraft to fly under B-29s and attack undetected. Night fighter *Hayate* did not carry radar, and relied on visual observation.

The Nakajima J1N1 *Gekkō* was one of three night fighters Japan used to defend Tokyo. It was too slow for more than one pass against a B-29, but it had the firepower to knock a B-29 out of the sky if the *Gekkō* had a proficient pilot. By 1945, those were rare. (AC)

Facilities and infrastructure

The physical area comprising "Tokyo" was massive. It stretched from Omiyo in the north to Yokosuka at the entrance of Tokyo Bay; from Hachiōji in the west to Chiba on the eastern shore of Tokyo Bay. The United States considered Tokyo all of that. The Japanese defense sector containing Tokyo contained still more area.

Within this area was 20 percent of Japan's total industrial output. It included 29 factories manufacturing aircraft, aircraft engines, or major aircraft subassemblies. It contained two major IJA arsenals and a major IJN one. Kawasaki and Yokohama held oil refineries, munitions factories, iron foundries, and steel plants. There were shipyards, motor vehicle plants, metal refineries, chemical plants, electrical products and electronics factories, and textile mills scattered throughout the urban complex.

Those were the big manufacturing facilities, the Japanese equivalents of the River Rouge complex or Bethlehem Steel plant. Throughout Tokyo were thousands of small machine shops, workshops, packing plants, and assembly shops. They were intermixed with residential areas, below or next to the homes of those who worked there. Small two- to five-man shops created parts and minor subassemblies that kept large factories supplied and running. As much as half of Tokyo's manufacturing capability came from these home workshops.

OPPOSITE TARGET TOKYO

The shoreline of Tokyo Bay, from Yokosuka to the northern limits of Tokyo, was lined with wharves, docks, and warehouses. Even Tokyo, furthest from the Pacific, could dock ships up to 10,000 tons. Up to 580 million tons of shipping flowed through these facilities every month. Yokohama by itself accounted for one-quarter of Japan's foreign prewar trade. Tokyo's commercial district directed the distribution of most goods in Japan, and was its banking hub.

This was the target to be defended. The first line of defense started over the Marianas. Whenever a B-29 strike was launched, the aircraft would test their radios. Interception stations in Japan picked up these transmissions, offering a five-hour warning when an attack was forthcoming. This did not reveal where it would occur, but it alerted the next step in the defense.

These were the early warning coastal radar stations guarding Japan's Pacific coast. The Imperial Army and Navy maintained their own chain of coastal stations. It duplicated effort and wasted scarce resources, but neither service trusted the other. Army radar had a range of 200km (124 miles), Navy radar 250km (155 miles). Japanese radar had several shortcomings. It did not provide aircraft altitude. It was easy to jam, as all Japanese radars used a narrow frequency spectrum. Imperial Army and Navy radar stations did not exchange information.

Thirteen stations provided early warning of attacks headed to Tokyo: four run by the Imperial Army and nine by the Imperial Navy. Three Navy radar stations were located on a set of 25 small islands scattered south from Tokyo Bay. Administratively, these islands were part of the city of Tokyo. The furthest from Tokyo was on Hachijō-Jima 228km (142 miles) south of Tokyo, positioned to detect incoming aircraft from the Marianas. It gave Tokyo an extra half-hour of warning.

Once the bombers were discovered inbound, whether Army Air Force or US Navy, a fighter response was triggered. Neither the Imperial Army nor Imperial Navy had organized ground control of its aircraft. The radar warnings were sent to the 16 airfields hosting fighter units.

Japan had developed radar systems by 1945. The Mark 4 radar was part of a family of radar sets used for searchlight control and antiaircraft fire control. It operated on a 1.5m wavelength. All Japanese radars used the same narrow spectrum of frequencies, which made them easy to jam. (AC)

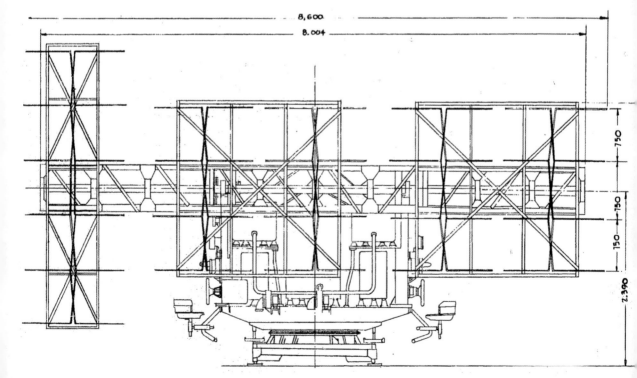

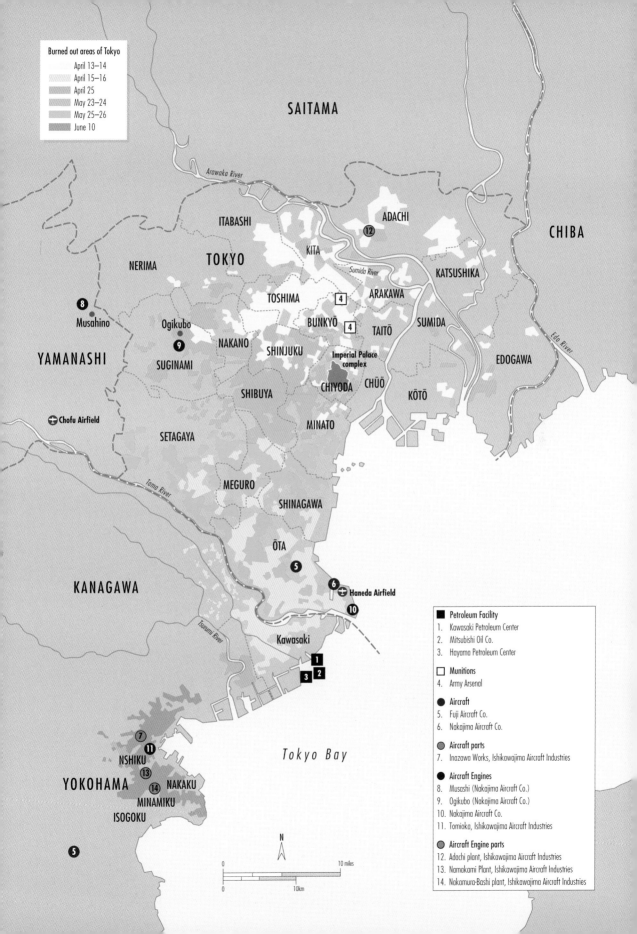

Burned out areas of Tokyo
- April 13–14
- April 15–16
- April 25
- May 23–24
- May 25–26
- June 10

SAITAMA

CHIBA

TOKYO

SAITAMA

Arawaka River

ITABASHI

ADACHI 12

NERIMA

KITA

TOSHIMA

Sumida River

KATSUSHIKA

Musahino 8

Ogikubo

ARAKAWA

SUMIDA

4

BUNKYŌ

4

TAITŌ

EDOGAWA

YAMANASHI

9

NAKANO

SHINJUKU

Imperial Palace
complex

Edo River

SUGINAMI

SHIBUYA

CHIYODA

CHŪŌ

KŌTŌ

MINATO

Chofu Airfield

SETAGAYA

Tama River

MEGURO

SHINAGAWA

ŌTA

KANAGAWA

5

Tsurumi River

6

Haneda Airfield

10

Kawasaki

1

2

3

7

11

NSHIKU

13

YOKOHAMA

14

NAKAKU

MINAMIKU

ISOGOKU

5

Tokyo Bay

N

0   10 miles

0   10km

■ Petroleum Facility
1. Kawasaki Petroleum Center
2. Mitsubishi Oil Co.
3. Hayama Petroleum Center

□ Munitions
4. Army Arsenal

● Aircraft
5. Fuji Aircraft Co.
6. Nakajima Aircraft Co.

● Aircraft parts
7. Inazawa Works, Ishikawajima Aircraft Industries

● Aircraft Engines
8. Musashi (Nakajima Aircraft Co.)
9. Ogikubo (Nakajima Aircraft Co.)
10. Nakajima Aircraft Co.
11. Tomioka, Ishikawajima Aircraft Industries

● Aircraft Engine parts
12. Adachi plant, Ishikawajima Aircraft Industries
13. Namakami Plant, Ishikawajima Aircraft Industries
14. Nakamura-Bashi plant, Ishikawajima Aircraft Industries

These were scattered in and around Tokyo proper, some far out on the Kantō Plain. Six were Imperial Army fields; nine belonged to the Imperial Navy, and one, Haneda Airfield, Tokyo's prewar commercial airfield, was shared by both services.

The final line of active defense was antiaircraft artillery. Japan had relatively little antiaircraft artillery, less than 7,000 guns of greater than 75mm bore in its entire empire. A significant fraction of that total, over 500 guns, protected the Tokyo urban complex. These guns were radar-directed, which improved accuracy, until the Army Air Force began deploying radar-jamming aircraft in April 1945. Jamming successfully forced batteries back to individual command and optical aiming.

Five hundred guns was an impressive total, but it was also scattered over an area 28 miles by 57 miles, 828 square miles in all. Guns were clustered in areas thought most important, such as aircraft factories, naval bases, shipyards, and airfields. Much of the urban complex was not covered by antiaircraft artillery or only lightly covered.

Tokyo's ultimate defense lay in civil defense. Tokyo's air-raid defense began in 1928. Between then and 1937, air-raid defense was solely the concern of the municipal government. Annual air-raid drills were held, which largely amounted to a demonstration held in cooperation with the Imperial Army and Navy. It was mainly to show Tokyo was a modern city, air-raid defense being the most modern problem a city faced in the 1920s and 1930s. The drills were more spectacular than scientific, and viewed as interesting but annoying.

Of the 6.7 million living within Tokyo's city limits in 1944, over 2.84 million were involved in the civil defense structure. Most, 2.7 million, belonged to Tokyo's 141,000 neighborhood groups and 4,000 block associations. These were unpaid positions.

Organized air-raid defense workers in Tokyo included 16,400 members of the police department, with responsibility for maintaining order, 8,100 professional firefighters, 16,000 medical personnel staffing Tokyo's 873 first aid stations and 472 first aid hospitals, 17,000 railroad personnel responsible for railroad air defense and repair, 3,244 emergency construction workers, 1,600 rescue workers, and 12,000 men responsible for disposal of the dead. During emergencies, the police were aided by 47,500 auxiliary policemen, while the fire department was supplemented by 8,600 auxiliary firemen and student volunteer firemen. Tokyo Bay, including Yokohama and Kawasaki, had a harbor firefighting contingent of 1,200-plus.

The weak link in this was firefighting. There were too few firefighters and far too few fire engines. The 8,100 firemen were 4,400 short of the planned staffing of 12,500 firefighters. Tokyo had only four ladder trucks, but only one worked. The Tokyo Fire Department had 839 pumper trucks with a 350- to 500-gallons-per-minute capacity. They were fitted with two hose reels carrying 2.5in linen hose. These were distributed among Tokyo's 42 main fire stations and 190 branch fire stations. A main station contained two pumpers and a branch station one. Standard procedure was to dispatch four pumpers to an alarm.

These were supplemented by hand-drawn fire pumps, some powered by engines capable of pumping 120 gallons per minute

Japanese antiaircraft artillery could reach the altitudes at which B-29s flew (9–10K), but this was near the ceiling for the most common antiaircraft artillery. This meant bombers had to fly almost directly over a gun position for the guns to reach it, since lateral range dropped quickly at maximum altitudes. (AC)

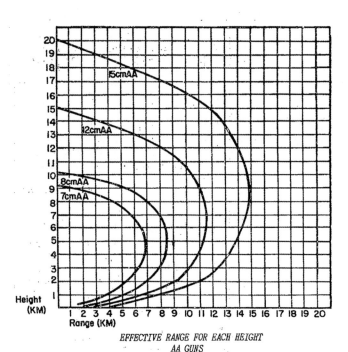

EFFECTIVE RANGE FOR EACH HEIGHT
AA GUNS

and some hand-operated pumps. Mechanized pumps were scattered throughout the city and at important factories, while hand-powered pumps were distributed among the block associations.

Tokyo had adequate water supplies, with a reservoir capacity of 80 million gallons and a total daily pumping capacity of 284 million gallons. Tokyo received 64in of rain annually, which, along with water fed by groundwater and nearby mountain rivers and lakes and its water system, kept the reservoirs filled. These supplied fire hydrants, over 33,650 in Tokyo proper. However, over 60 percent of these drew water from mains 4in in diameter or less, restricting their capacity. Because fire posed serious danger in residential areas, each dwelling had a 30- to 50-gallon concrete water tank to combat small fires.

Civil defense played an important role in the campaign for Tokyo. In addition to firefighting, civil defense was responsible for search and rescue of those trapped in bombed-out buildings. Tokyo had only 21,000 police, emergency construction workers, and rescue workers to deal with air raids, too few for a city of 8 million. (Wikimedia)

Weapons and tactics

Japan used two categories of weapons to defend their cities: weapons carried aboard the aircraft defending Tokyo and antiaircraft artillery. Aircraft weapons fell into three broad categories: machine guns, cannon, and air-to-air bombs. Two calibers of machine guns were used: the 7.7mm machine gun (equivalent to American .30 caliber or British .303 machine guns) and 12.7mm (.50 caliber) machine gun. Japanese aircraft defending Tokyo also carried 20mm, 30mm, and 37mm cannon.

The 7.9mm was a rifle-caliber gun, dating to World War I. Two types were used, the Army's Type 89 and the Navy's Type 97 machine guns. Both were licensed copies of the British Vickers .303 machine guns; they were chambered for different cartridges which could not be interchanged. They were mounted on early-war fighters and the *Hien*, typically in the nose of the aircraft, synchronized to fire through the propeller arc. They fired bullets too light to reliably destroy multi-engine US bombers, especially the robust B-29.

Late-war Army fighters replaced the 7.7mm machine gun with the heavier Ho-103 12.7mm (.50 caliber) machine gun. An unauthorized copy of the Browning M2 machine

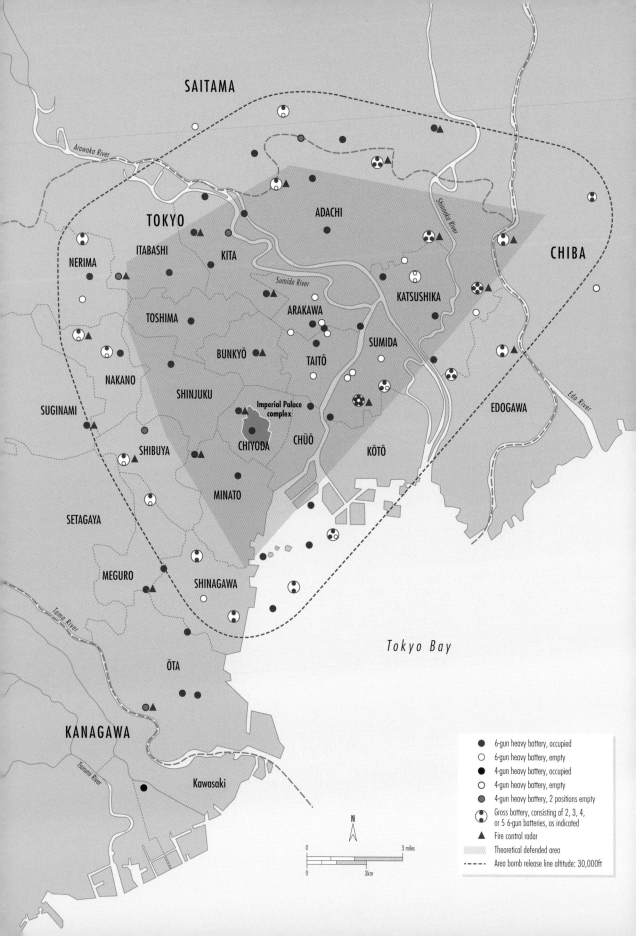

SAITAMA

Arawaka River

TOKYO

ADACHI

Shinnaka River

CHIBA

ITABASHI

KITA

NERIMA

Sumida River

KATSUSHIKA

TOSHIMA

ARAKAWA

SUMIDA

BUNKYŌ

TAITŌ

NAKANO

Imperial Palace
complex

SHINJUKU

SUGINAMI

CHIYODA

CHŪŌ

EDOGAWA

Edo River

SHIBUYA

KŌTŌ

MINATO

SETAGAYA

MEGURO

SHINAGAWA

Tokyo Bay

ŌTA

KANAGAWA

Tama River

Tsurumi River

Kawasaki

N

0   3 miles

0   3km

● 6-gun heavy battery, occupied
○ 6-gun heavy battery, empty
● 4-gun heavy battery, occupied
○ 4-gun heavy battery, empty
● 4-gun heavy battery, 2 positions empty
⊛ Gross battery, consisting of 2, 3, 4,
   or 5 6-gun batteries, as indicated
▲ Fire control radar
▨ Theoretical defended area
--- Area bomb release line altitude: 30,000ft

OPPOSITE TOKYO'S AA ARTILLERY DEFENSES

gun, it was introduced in 1941. It had a higher rate of fire than the M2, through use of a shorter cartridge. This gave it a shorter range. Effective against single-engine Allied aircraft, it was less so against large multi-engine bombers.

The Japanese used a variety of aerial cannon. Early-war Zeroes had two wing-mounted, low-velocity Type 99 Mark 1 20mm cannon, with a low muzzle velocity and a 60-round magazine. This was adequate against carrier aircraft, but not against the B-29. The Imperial Navy moved to the Type 99 Mark 2, 20mm with a high muzzle velocity and 100-round magazine. Imperial Army aircraft used Ho-1, Ho-3 (developed from an anti-tank gun), and Ho-5 20mm cannon. The Ho-5 was developed from the Ho-103 machine gun, essentially a Browning M2 up-gunned to an autocannon. Imperial Army twin-engine fighters carried Ho-203 and Ho-204 30mm cannon, fitted as nose guns and also had fixed upward-firing guns in night fighters.

Due to the light armament of their fighters, the Imperial Army and Navy attempted to use air-to-air bombs against bomber formations. Several types were used. The simplest was to fuse conventional bombs to explode in mid-air. This required the attacking aircraft to fly a prescribed height above a bomber formation so the bomb exploded among them. Both Army and Navy developed scattering bombs, with 30 to 76 contact-fused bomblets loaded into a container. This opened after being dropped, scattering the bomblets. Each bomblet-held .33kg (.74lb) explosive charge exploded on contact. A single hit would do serious damage to a Superfortress. They also developed a parachute bomb and a cable bomb; however, neither became operational. All operational air-to-air bombs experienced targeting problems.

Antiaircraft fell into two broad categories: heavy and light. Heavy antiaircraft guns were those with a bore in excess of 75mm. Light antiaircraft guns were either machine guns or 20mm and 25mm cannon. Heavy antiaircraft guns were effective primarily against medium- to high-altitude-level bombers. Their shells were fused to explode at a preset altitude, reducing effectiveness against low-level attack or dive- and glide-bombing attack. Light antiaircraft had a high rate of fire, which made them useful against diving attacks and low-level attacks. They were fused to explode on impact, with the weight of fire increasing the chance of getting a hit.

Light antiaircraft was ineffective against B-29 raids. Their effective ceiling was 4,000 to 5,000ft, below that flown by B-29. They primarily saw service protecting airfields around

The Japanese equipped night fighters with upward firing and downward firing cannon. The fighters could sneak up behind a B-29 and attack it from above or below with these guns. Since the night fighter was not moving directly towards the bomber, the bomber's crew sometimes failed to spot the fighter and got shot down. (AC)

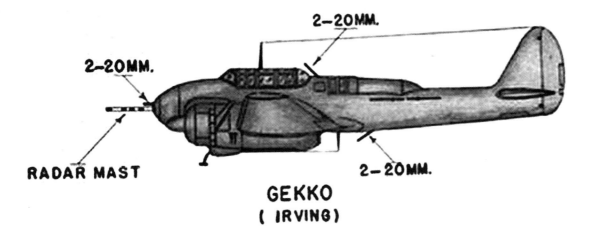

2-20MM.

2-20MM.

2-20MM.

RADAR MAST

GEKKO
(IRVING)

OPPOSITE WAYS TO ATTACK UNESCORTED B-29S

Tokyo rather than industrial or harbor facilities. The high-flying B-29s provided a major challenge to heavy antiaircraft artillery. Only four Japanese antiaircraft guns had a maximum vertical range at or above 30,000ft: the Imperial Army Model 14 105mm and Model 88 75mm guns, and the Imperial Navy's 120mm/45 and Model 89 127mm guns. All four had an effective ceiling below 27,000ft, which meant B-29 formations had to fly almost directly over one of these to be at any risk.

Most tactics used focused on aerial interception of air raids, whether conducted by single-engine aircraft or B-29 bombers. Defense started with radar detection of incoming enemy aircraft. Through April 1945, radar stations would notify airfields of their service (Army or Navy) of an incoming strike, providing the location when detected and the direction they were flying.

The information was passed on to aircraft at the airfield, which would scramble to intercept the enemy aircraft. Once aloft, the aircraft were on their own, hunting the intruders visually or (if the aircraft were so equipped) with radar. During daylight hours, this was usually effective enough to find the enemy. US Navy aircraft were generally hunting Japanese aircraft. They made themselves easy to locate. Large daytime B-29 formations were easy to spot and rarely used indirect paths to their targets.

The difficulty Japanese fighters had in shooting down enough B-29s led the Imperial Army and Navy to experiment with air-to-air bombs. These were to be dropped on B-29 formations and explode among them. This cluster munition was one type of air-to-air bomb the Imperial Navy developed. It proved almost totally ineffective. (AC)

Finding targets was more difficult during the nights' limited visibility and frequent failure of airborne radar. The B-29s flew individually, spaced 45 seconds apart. Night fighters had to find the bomber stream and hope to pick up aircraft on that path. Historically, Japanese night fighters proved incapable of that task.

Having found the enemy, the goal was engaging them. By late 1944, Japanese fighters operated in teams of four aircraft, with two sections of two aircraft. One pilot led; and the second served as a wingman. These often broke up during combat, especially when engaging enemy fighters. When engaging single-engine aircraft, the Japanese preferred to attack from above and behind. Due to the light build of most Japanese fighters, they generally lost head-on exchanges with US fighters.

To attack B-29s in daylight combat formations, the Japanese developed specialized tactics. Any B-29 leaving the formation became a target. It was safer to attack a lone B-29 than a formation. It could be swarmed. Against B-29s in formation, the preferred attack was from ahead. Due to the B-29's high speed, a rear attack resulted in a slow approach against the massed guns of a formation.

NAVY

← 219 MM →

1086 MM

60 KG. NO. 21 BOMB
2 STYLE-2

(CYLINDRICAL CONTAINER
HOUSES 36 BABY BOMBS)

← 60 MM →

290 MM

IMPACT FUSE

BOOSTER

H.E.

BABY BOMB

Ways to attack unescorted B-29s

The two best ways were to attack from ahead of the formation of B-29s: (1) From ahead and well above, diving on the B-29, aiming for the bomb-bay and fuel tanks. (2) From ahead and slightly below, aiming down the length of the aircraft.
The worst way was from behind, a slow approach that gave gunners plenty of time to shoot you down.

Overhead attack

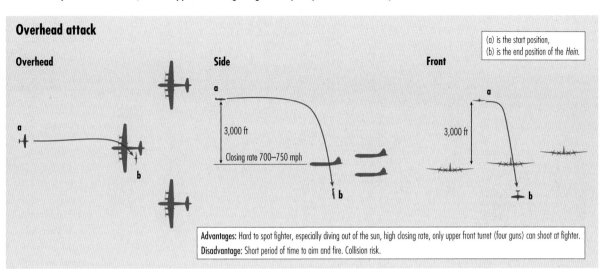

(a) is the start position,
(b) is the end position of the *Hein*.

Overhead   **Side**   **Front**

3,000 ft

Closing rate 700–750 mph

3,000 ft

Advantages: Hard to spot fighter, especially diving out of the sun, high closing rate, only upper front turret (four guns) can shoot at fighter.
Disadvantage: Short period of time to aim and fire. Collision risk.

Head-on, below attack

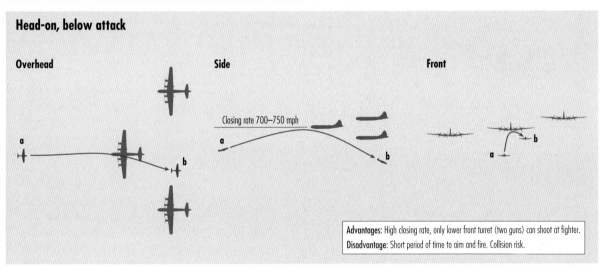

Overhead   **Side**   **Front**

Closing rate 700–750 mph

Advantages: High closing rate, only lower front turret (two guns) can shoot at fighter.
Disadvantage: Short period of time to aim and fire. Collision risk.

Stern attack

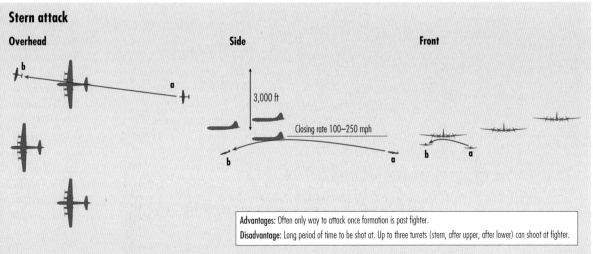

Overhead   **Side**   **Front**

3,000 ft

Closing rate 100–250 mph

Advantages: Often only way to attack once formation is past fighter.
Disadvantage: Long period of time to be shot at. Up to three turrets (stern, after upper, after lower) can shoot at fighter.

Desperate to destroy B-29s, the 10th Air Division formed a volunteer unit, the 244th Sentai, to conduct "special assault" tactics – ramming B-29s with modified *Hien*. This diagram illustrates the method used in a ramming attack. After the collision, the pilot was expected to bail out so they could fly future missions with new aircraft. (AC)

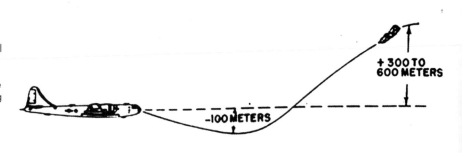

BELLY APPROACH FROM AHEAD OF TARGET.

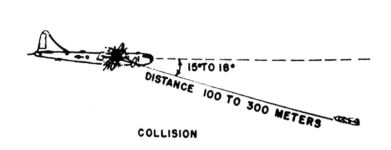

COLLISION

Two types of frontal attacks were used, frontal overhead and nose attack. In a frontal overhead attack, the fighter approached from ahead, 1,000yds above the B-29 formation. The fighter then dove on the targeted bomber when overhead. A nose attack began ahead of and slightly below the targeted B-29. Both minimized the effectiveness of the bomber's defensive guns. Gunners found it difficult to engage an aircraft diving straight down, and attacking the nose from below meant only the forward lower turret could fire at the attacking fighter.

Night fighter tactics were the opposite to those of the day fighters. The optimal night fighter attack was to come from behind, below the B-29, moving undetected until the fighter was under the bomber. Then it would fire, aiming at the region of the bomb bay. A successful attack almost inevitably destroyed the bomber. Success depended on not being detected. A B-29 could speed up and almost outrun a Japanese night fighter. Additionally, the B-29s were equipped with both radar and radar-jamming equipment, making it difficult for night fighters to find their prey.

Japan also used "special attack" or ramming tactics against B-29s. These used specially prepared *Hien* fighters. Upon warning, these aircraft took off. Upon finding a B-29 formation, the aircraft made a frontal pass at the target B-29. The aiming point was the wing between the B-29's fuselage and inner engine. After hitting the B-29, the pilot bailed out, if possible. Although ramming was infrequent, some Japanese pilots made multiple successful attacks before finally dying.

CAMPAIGN OBJECTIVES
The high-stakes target

No target in Japan was as important as Tokyo. The United States saw its destruction as critical on many levels. It was the largest industrial center in Japan, rivaled only by Nagoya. Tokyo was Japan's largest city and the urban area around Tokyo had Japan's largest population concentration. It was Japan's political capital and its cultural and commercial capital. Every reason its destruction was sought by the United States was a reason for Japan to preserve it.

That made this campaign a zero-sum game. Every point the US scored towards Tokyo's destruction was a point Japan lost. Japan won by preventing their opponent from achieving their goal. Equally, as long as the destruction wreaked by US aircraft, Army Air Force or US Navy, was greater than the cost in material and personnel resources suffered by the attacking aircraft, US losses would not deter further attack by the US. For both sides the objective was simple: they lose, we win.

That meant inflicting losses on the enemy. If Japan could shoot down US aircraft (especially the high-tech and resource-intensive B-29) faster than they could be replaced, the US would have to abandon its campaign against Tokyo. If the US could destroy Tokyo's manufacturing, financial, and communications value faster than Japan could repair the damage, Tokyo would cease being an engine in Japan's military machine. Achieving their objectives required developing the right plans.

For the Allies, it was not a simple matter of dumping enough high explosives on Tokyo. It was too large to turn the entire city into rubble using high-altitude precision bombing. Instead, it had to identify the high-value targets, put them on the target list in order of importance, and bomb them. Bombing a target was not the same thing as destroying it. To destroy it, the bombs had to hit the target, with bombs large enough to destroy it. Due to logistics limitations, the US could not afford overkill. Success required planning that made effective and economical use of US resources.

For the Japanese, it meant effectively intercepting the US aircraft heading to Tokyo and shooting them down in sufficient numbers to deter further attacks, with the limited resources available. It also meant minimizing the damage raids did through effective civil defense

A flight of Helldivers from the Essex-class carrier *Lexington* off the coast of Japan in February 1945. The US Navy was coming off a successful raid into the South China Sea as February started. They saw attacking Tokyo as a means of demonstrating the reach and power of US Navy aviation. (USNHHC)

measures. This was not an impossible task, especially early on in the campaign. Had Japan caused sufficient casualties then, the Army Air Force might have been forced to abandon its strategic bombing campaign and turn over control of the B-29s to theater commanders. Achieving that goal required the right plans.

The Japanese defenders of Tokyo had one advantage over their US attackers. For the US, Tokyo was just one target in an overall strategic campaign against Japan. For the Japanese, Tokyo *was* Japan. It got first priority on resources. It had more of everything – population, civil defense, fire trucks, antiaircraft guns, radar warning – than any other city in Japan. As they accumulated losses in equipment to defend Tokyo, they could call on more from other parts of the country. The US could do that only at the expenses of their campaign against greater Japan.

Allied objectives and plans

The aerial destruction of Tokyo was part of two larger campaigns run by the Army Air Force and US Navy. Both viewed the reduction of Tokyo as a critical part of a larger strategic campaign. It was an element within the Army Air Force's overall strategic bombing campaign against Japan. It was seen by the US Navy as a means of projecting power on the Japanese Home Islands as a precursor to an ultimate land invasion of Japan. The efforts were run independently by the two services, although they coordinated.

For the Army Air Force, the strategic bombing of Japan was an opportunity to realize a dream air power supporters had advocated for over 20 years: to demonstrate air power alone could defeat an industrialized nation. That armies and navies were obsolete because aircraft could overfly them. Strategic bombers could attack and destroy a nation's vital centers – governmental centers, industry, and transportation networks. Collapse would follow, resulting in victory.

The B-29 was developed for this purpose. It flew higher, faster, and further than any other bomber, while carrying a significant bombload. Its range was so great that from its inception, the Army Air Force viewed it as a purely strategic asset. The B-29s were organized into an air force independent of theater commanders, reporting directly to Army Air Force headquarters in Washington, D.C.

To attack Japan, the Army Air Force created the Twentieth Air Force. Initial plans called for the XX Bomber Command to attack Japan from China, while the XXI would mount raids from the Marianas. Five B-29 wings were organized, with one intended to operate out of China, three from the Marianas, and one from Luzon in the Philippines. Logistics difficulties shut down China operations after a few months. B-29 bases were never built in the Philippines. The wing in China and the wing intended for the Philippines were sent to the Marianas.

Japan seemed perfect for a demonstration of air power. It was an island nation. Japan was a major industrial nation, with the second largest

A formation of B-29s heading towards Japan. The B-29 represented the culmination of a dream held by air power advocates for over 20 years: winning wars through air power alone. It had never been done before, but given Japan's position as an island nation, Army Air Force leaders believed the B-29 could achieve that. (NMAF)

economy of the Axis nations. It was viewed as a perfect laboratory for a controlled experiment on air power. If the theory of strategic bombardment worked, it eliminated the need for a costly ground invasion of Japan. Right up until landing day, Japan could only be attacked by air power. With few exceptions, invading Japanese-held territory proved bloody for Allied troops. Japanese soldiers fought tenaciously, dying rather than surrendering.

If strategic bombing yielded the promised victory, it avoided a bloody ground campaign. Most of the dead would be Japanese, not Allied airmen, sailors, and soldiers. When the Army Air Force began planning its strategic campaign against Japan in late 1943, the earliest projected date for an invasion of the Home Islands was 1947. "Golden Gate in '48" – meaning a return to California in 1948 following a victorious Allied invasion of Japan – was what ground pounders in the Pacific were then saying.

The capture of the Marianas in the summer of 1944 put Japan within range of B-29s. Even then, Allied planners expected to invade Japan no sooner than late fall of 1945. Most thought it would not occur until 1946. Army Air Force planners realized they had at least a year to defeat Japan using air power. They were determined to demonstrate it was enough to force Japan's surrender.

The Army Air Force planned targeting six different Japanese industries. In order: aircraft plants (including aircraft motors), petroleum refineries, iron and steel production, electronics, and antifriction bearings. Destroy those and you would destroy Japan's war-making ability. Aircraft production and petroleum topped the list. Without aircraft Japan could not stop Allied air power. Without fuel they could not fly their aircraft, steam their warships, or move their armies.

When the strategic air campaign started, it was based in China. It focused on iron and steel production, the targets in Japan most accessible to Chinese airfields. With the capture of the Marianas, emphasis shifted to aircraft factories. Aircraft production was clustered in Honshu, on Japan's Pacific coast, readily reached from the Marianas. Petroleum slipped down the list because Japan imported most of the oil it refined and the US Navy was preventing oil from reaching Japanese refineries.

A home factory in Tokyo. Much of Japan's industrial base rested on small manufacturing plants co-located in the residences of the owners and employees. This food packing plant was typical of the small factories in Tokyo. Precision bombing was ill-suited to attacking these. Area bombing was effective but contrary to Army Air Force doctrine. (AC)

These targets were to be attacked using precision bombing. Initially, this required daylight raids, with the bombers in a tight formation for mutual protection. As improved radar came into service, precision bombing could be conducted at night. Those missions, given Japan's poor night fighter capabilities, did not require formation flying for mutual protection. High-altitude precision bombing was viewed as the key to success. Low- and medium-altitude bombing failed to use the B-29's ability to fight at altitudes difficult for Japanese fighters and antiaircraft artillery to reach. Area bombing was initially dismissed. It clashed with the Army Air Force's vision of surgical destruction of the enemy.

Area bombing proved ineffective in reducing Germany's war production, something Army Air Force air power advocates recognized, even as they ignored that precision daylight bombing had been almost as ineffective as area bombing. Differences between Germany and Japan were initially ignored. In Germany, the target of area bombing was the "dormitory zones," the section where workers lived, rather than the factories where they worked. Houses burned better than large factories, but burning out workers' housing did not prevent them from continuing to work in their largely undamaged factories.

In Japan, a significant fraction of its production came from home manufacturing shops, small factories, and machine shops that produced component subassemblies for larger factories. Destroy component production and the large factories halted production. These home factories were interspersed with residential housing. In most cases, workers lived next to or above their workplace. Most buildings were of wood construction, filled with combustible material. They were also highly concentrated, close together, with narrow alleys separating buildings. Although incendiary area bombing was initially ignored, the opportunity it offered was eventually used.

For the US Navy, attacking the Home Islands was a way to demonstrate naval carrier air power was as capable of conducting a sustained strategic bombing campaign as the Army Air Force. By late 1944, its Fast Carrier Force routinely fielded 1,000 or more aircraft. In January 1945, it conducted a three-week rampage in the South China Sea. It swept the seas of Japanese shipping and the skies of Japanese aircraft.

For the rest of the war, it steamed along Japanese-held coasts with the intention of hunting down Japanese warships and luring remaining Japanese warplanes into confrontations with US Navy aircraft. This included several sweeps along the Home Islands.

Tokyo was an integral part of both services' air campaign against the Home Islands. The Tokyo urban area, with three of Japan's ten largest cities, was a population hub. It held the second largest concentration of Japan's aviation industry (only Nagoya held more). As Japan's Imperial capital, it held tremendous symbolic value. Its destruction – or rather, in the US Armed Forces' view, the destruction of its industrial and military capability – would go a long way to furthering Allied victory if an invasion were required. It might even contribute to an invasion being unnecessary.

While the Twentieth Air Force bombed cities in Kyushu from China, Tokyo was the first daylight precision attack it made

Brigadier General Haywood Hansell and the staff of the XXI Bomber Command plan a mission to Tokyo in 1944. They viewed Tokyo as Japan's most challenging and most important target. Destroying Tokyo was seen as a step on the path to Allied victory, but attacking it without incurring excessive losses required careful planning. (AC)

on the Home Islands. The attack was mounted from the Marianas. Tokyo would prove the Twentieth Air Force's main target over the next seven months of the war. Tokyo's size made multiple missions inevitable.

The Army Air Force's initial attack strategy was to start with the target in Tokyo assigned the highest strategic value, destroy it, and work down the list of strategic targets by assigned priority. Once the bottom of the list was reached, Tokyo could be scratched from the target list. The Twentieth Air Force expected to revisit targets due to insufficient damage on earlier raids or to undo Japanese repair efforts. Yet it felt reasonably certain it could neutralize Tokyo within six months.

High-altitude precision bombing over Japan proved survivable. It could be conducted with acceptable losses, even without fighter escort. Initially, it proved ineffective. Not enough bombs landed on the target, requiring multiple raids on the same factories. Between November 24, 1944 and March 4, 1945, the Twentieth Air Force made 20 high-altitude raids on Japan. Eleven targeted Tokyo, over half the missions flown.

They only chipped away at Tokyo. The lack of results led to the relief of the XXI Bomber Command's original commander, Brigadier General Haywood S. "Possum" Hansell, Jr. He was replaced on January 20 by the former head of XX Bomber Command, Major General Curtis LeMay. LeMay instituted a new plan, not just for Tokyo, but for the entire campaign. High-altitude precision bombing would be augmented by medium-level, nighttime incendiary attacks. LeMay viewed this as attacking Tokyo's industrial capacity due to the contribution home industries made to Japan's war economy. As with precision bombing, Tokyo would be the first place this was attempted.

Japanese objectives and plans

For the Imperial Army and Navy, and the civil authorities in the Tokyo urban complex, the defense of Tokyo went beyond military duty. Tokyo was the home of Japan's Emperor. He was more than a monarch. To the Japanese, he was a deity, the most recent in an unbroken string of god-kings that stretched 2,500 years into the past. Tokyo's defense was a sacred responsibility. The objective of the military was to prevent Tokyo from being attacked. The objective of the civil authorities was to minimize the damage done when attacked.

The military responsibility for Tokyo's defense was held by the Eastern District Army. Headquartered in Tokyo, it ran the defense of Kantō and Northern Honshu. It controlled the 12th Area Army, tasked with the direct defense of Tokyo. Even before invasion became a serious threat in 1945, most of the focus of these commands was ground defense of Tokyo. It also held responsibility for Tokyo's aerial defense.

Two of its subordinate units were heavily involved with that: the 10th Flying Division and the 1st Anti-Aircraft Artillery Brigade. The former controlled Imperial Army aircraft within the Eastern District Army's region. The latter, part of the 12th Area Army, provided antiaircraft protection for the Tokyo urban area. Both were headquartered in Tokyo.

The Yokosuka Naval District held responsibility for protecting Tokyo Bay and the waters around it from naval threats. Its aerial component was the Imperial Navy's 302nd Air Group. Additionally, it had antiaircraft artillery elements guarding Imperial Navy assets.

Military plans to defend Tokyo were rudimentary and reactive; detect enemy aircraft as early as possible, then launch fighters to shoot down the attackers, whether B-29s and their escorting fighters, or US Navy aircraft. Antiaircraft artillery would deal with any attackers that got past the fighters. With roughly 120 fighters and 500 antiaircraft guns available, it was too numerically small to deal with a major air raid – 120 or more enemy aircraft.

That was the best case, assuming the resources available were used efficiently. They were not. The Imperial Army and Navy ran separate efforts. The two services did not coordinate early warning information, dispatching of aircraft, or placement of antiaircraft guns.

Shizuichi Tanaka took command of Japan's Eastern District Army on March 9, 1945, the day before the March 10 fire raid that devastated Tokyo. Both the 10th Air Division and the 1st Anti-Aircraft Artillery Brigade tasked with defending Tokyo belonged to the Eastern District Army. From its headquarters in Tokyo, Shizuichi guided Tokyo's defense until the war ended. (Wikimedia)

They each communicated with the rival service poorly, and refused to take orders from their rival.

Britain and Germany organized integrated air defense systems. They established central control centers which dispatched interceptors to incoming attackers, directing them until they made contact. Japan did not. Instead, radar information was sent to individual airfields. The local squadron commander held responsibility for launching his aircraft and directing his pilots towards the enemy. That typically meant bomber formations were not met by a single massed attack by all interceptors available that day, but rather by a series of unit attacks, with ten to 50 aircraft in each attack.

The information provided pilots was rudimentary, such as bearing and distance of the enemy formations. Once aloft, there was little further guidance. It was not difficult to find B-29 formations, at least during daylight missions. It was difficult to place fighter groups in a good position to attack lacking ground vectoring. If fighters were below the formation, it often meant the B-29s flew beyond the fighters before they could gain altitude. Night fighters were in an even worse plight. They had to use their onboard radar to detect targets and their radar lacked identification friend or foe (IFF).

The result was the enemy always reached their target. Not without loss, but throughout the air campaign B-29 combat losses were never high enough to deter daylight raids, even before fighter escort became available. When the bombers arrived, defense of Tokyo became the concern of its civil authorities. They focused on minimizing damage done by raids.

Tokyo had one of the biggest and most comprehensive civil defense systems in Japan; possibly the world. It predated the Pacific War, and even the rise of the military aircraft, with roots in feudal Japan. It emerged in its modern form after the 1923 Great Kantō earthquake which flattened Tokyo and Yokohama. Earthquake response and air-raid damage response required many parallel skills. Fire was an eternal threat to Japanese cities, especially one as built-up as the Tokyo urban complex. Earthquakes and air raids created similar challenges of dealing with fires in a rubble-filled environment. In the 1930s, when the threat posed by aircraft grew large enough, air defense response and earthquake response were merged.

In April 1937, when the Second Sino-Japanese War began, a national civilian air defense law was passed. It created a national air defense authority, with municipal offices. This removed authority from cities, assigning them to the prefecture. The Tokyo Prefecture (which included the entire urban area around Tokyo) became responsible for planning and administration of air-raid policy. It created a competing bureaucracy with the municipal governments. This confused air-raid planning. This confusion was compounded because the municipal police, critical in air defense, reported to the national Ministry of Home Affairs, not to the prefecture or municipal government. They placed higher priority on protecting their administrative turf than in cooperating with other organizations.

By 1943, the conflict between the city government, prefectural government, and police became so notorious, the Imperial government stepped in. It created a metropolitan government (similar to the District of Columbia in the US) combining the administrative authority of all three, replacing the municipal and prefectural government. The metropolitan district, *Tokyo-Tu*, was broken into eight bureaus, including a bureau of defense responsible for air-raid defense over the whole area. The police board was reorganized and became the metropolitan police. The change did not stop the police from ignoring the *Tokyo-Tu* air-raid authority unless convenient. Thus, there were two air-raid programs in *Tokyo-Tu*, the civilian administration and the police.

Neighborhood groups were built around ten-family teams which regulated life in Japan. These dated to feudal Japan, and served as a form of social control, a precursor to today's social credit system. These groups held local-level responsibility for fire prevention and control. Air-raid defense was rolled into fire prevention. Two members of each group were elected leaders by the families in the group, one as the group leader, the other as the air-raid defense leader. Both held responsibility for leading firefighting, conducting blackout control, spreading air-raid warnings, and guiding members to shelter during air raids. They had little training and little equipment. Typical firefighting equipment consisted of buckets, filled by neighborhood water cisterns and sand piles.

Block associations were originally voluntary mutual-assistance clubs, with dues collected. These were used to improve the neighborhood; the association might hire a night watchman. In 1937, the government made membership mandatory, and subordinated neighborhood groups to the block association. The government appointed leaders for these groups, who appointed two assistant leaders. By 1944, this association had a defense section with responsibilities for air-raid warning and firefighting. The defense section had three to four

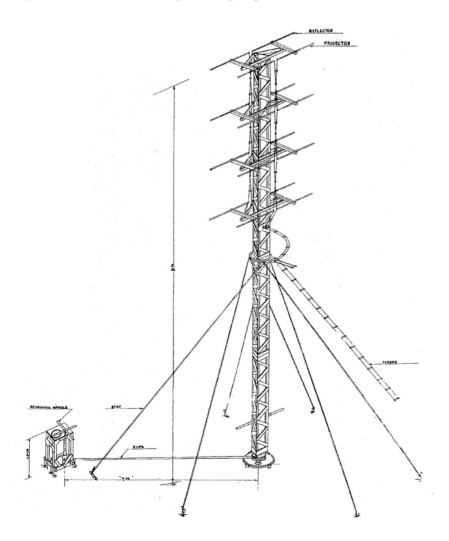

The antenna for a Japanese Type 3, Mark 1, Model 3 radar. Serving as a long-range search radar, it used a 2m wave and had a maximum range of 300km. This design was used by the Imperial Japanese Navy. These radars guarded the eastern approaches to Tokyo. Some were located on the Izu Islands. (AC)

hand-pumps for firefighting, which were often assigned to neighborhood groups within the block association's territory.

Firefighting at this low level was critical in Japan, even in peacetime. Housing was lightly built and highly combustible, with charcoal braziers used for heating and cooking. Stopping fires before they spread was critical. In wartime, a group member with a bucket of sand could douse an M-69 or M-74 incendiary before it spread its flames.

Every factory, public building, office building, and theater had a self-defense unit, a *bogodan,* made up of the employees of the building. One-fifth of a factory's workers might be part of its *bogodan*, while all employees of a theater belonged to it. These men conducted air-raid defense, including firefighting within facilities, whenever an air raid occurred.

Backing these up was Tokyo's fire department. Although undermanned (firefighters could and were drafted into the military), they could respond to as many as 70 fires too large to be contained by neighborhood groups and block associations. Fireboats in Tokyo Bay could handle up to eight waterfront fires. This limit assumed the fires were reached quickly and kept from spreading. A combination of alarm boxes and watch towers, combined with a central dispatching system that received their alerts and fire reports called in by telephone, were used to send trucks to calls. Alarm boxes were electrically powered, and ceased working if electricity failed.

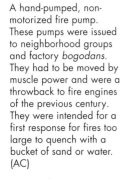

A hand-pumped, non-motorized fire pump. These pumps were issued to neighborhood groups and factory *bogodans*. They had to be moved by muscle power and were a throwback to fire engines of the previous century. They were intended for a first response for fires too large to quench with a bucket of sand or water. (AC)

Tokyo was rebuilt after the Great Kantō earthquake with wide avenues and large open parks. The avenues were intended to serve as firebreaks and the open areas as havens from the large conflagrations that inevitably followed earthquakes. When it became evident Tokyo would be subject to air attack, civil authorities expanded this protection. They created 78 miles of firebreaks, demolishing thousands of structures to clear 120ft to 300ft lanes through densely built sections of Tokyo.

Civil authorities acquired and stored emergency stocks of food, medical supplies, clothing, and fuel prior to the raids, and evacuated schoolchildren and the elderly from Tokyo. They developed plans for emergency response during raids and relief activities following them. All air defense plans were scaled for the maximum air raids Imperial Japan could mount; what could be expected was 100 to perhaps 200 twin-engine medium bombers.

THE CAMPAIGN

To destroy a capital

The Doolittle Raid was a false dawn. Another 31 months passed before US bombers again appeared in Tokyo skies. The campaign resumed when US forces invaded the Marianas on June 15, 1944. US soldiers and marines landed on Saipan, the seat of Japan's colonial government in the Marianas. A month later, US forces recaptured Guam, a prewar US territory taken by Japan in 1941, and captured Tinian, another Japanese mandate island in the Marianas.

Because of its role as an administrative center, Saipan had a major airfield, capable of handling long-range aircraft. It formed part of an airfield network allowing Japanese warplanes to shuttle throughout the Pacific. There was also a prewar airfield on Guam, built by the United States. During the war, Japan built other airfields on those islands to support their war effort. The capture of Saipan, Guam, and Tinian gave those airfields to the US. Their new owners immediately began expanding those airfields to accommodate B-29s.

Although recapturing Guam and cutting off the Japanese bastion at Truk were factors in taking the Marianas, the B-29 was the major reason. From Marianas bases they could reach Japan, including Tokyo. The Japanese realized this, too. Following Saipan's capture, Japan's government collapsed, replaced by a "peace" government. Its goal was ending the war Japan was losing without conceding defeat.

It took four months of airfield construction before B-29s could begin operating from the Marianas. Construction continued for additional months to permit five B-29 wings to operate from there. On October 12, the first B-29 landed at Isley Field in Saipan. Over the next month, the US accumulated B-29s and prepared to launch an air offensive against Japan. Tokyo was a major focus. Tokyo, in turn, prepared its reception for this aerial onslaught.

A formation of B-29s flies over Mount Fuji. The conical and symmetric volcanic cone is Japan's tallest mountain. One of Japan's Three Holy Mountains, Fuji is an unmistakable landmark, and US bombers used it as a navigational waypoint and as a rendezvous target when the Twentieth Air Force attacked Tokyo. (NMAF)

Opening salvos: November 1–January 9, 1945

On November 1, 1944, a lone four-engine aircraft appeared in the skies over Tokyo. It was the first enemy aircraft over Tokyo since April 18, 1942, when Doolittle's B-25s struck.

The first raid on Tokyo

On November 24, 1944, the XXI Bomber Command launched the first air attack on Tokyo since the Doolittle Raid. The target was Nakajima's Musashino Aircraft Engine Factory, 10 miles west of Tokyo. Of the 110 B-29s sent, only 24 bombed the primary target. The rest aborted or bombed secondary targets.

Key:

— Japanese aircraft
— US aircraft

6

7

EVENTS

1. 73rd Wing aircraft reach Mt. Fuji rendezvous and turn to the Musashi Factory.

2. Japanese fighters begin to intercept bomber formation.

3. 24 B-29s visually bomb Musashi Factory, doing minor damage.

4. Remaining B-29s bomb secondary targets in Tokyo docks and industrial areas.

5. Japanese fighters break off attacks on B-29s.

6. One B-29, damaged by ramming, crashes into the Pacific.

7. Remaining B-29s return to Saipan.

One of Tokyo's 42 main fire stations. This was a large fire station. It contains a firewatch tower and is capable of housing up to four engines. Although this station has three engines, most only had two. The engines were small, capable of pumping only 500gpm. (AC)

The Japanese assumed it was a B-29. In reality, it was an F-13A, the photoreconnaissance version of the B-29. Outwardly indistinguishable from the bomber, the F-13A was armed with cameras and electronic countermeasure equipment (ECM), not bombs. This aircraft, from the 3rd Photo Reconnaissance Squadron of the 73rd Bombardment Wing, arrived in Saipan two days earlier.

It spent 35 minutes circling the Tokyo urban area at 32,000ft. The day was clear, one of the few perfect days that month. The aircraft, appropriately named *Tokyo Rose*, returned to Saipan unmolested, with 7,000 photos of the Tokyo environs. Over the next three weeks, 3rd PRS flew 17 single-plane missions over Japan, including eight weather reconnaissance flights. Neither Japanese flak nor its fighters proved effective against these flights. Even heavy flak did no damage, while fighters found it almost impossible to get close enough to engage the swift recon aircraft. The only problem these aircraft encountered was the weather. Many flights were hampered by bad weather.

Perhaps because of the inability of Japanese interceptors to engage the intruders, on November 7 the 10th Flying Division created a flight to conduct ramming tactics against the B-29s. A flight in the 244th Fighter Group was designated as a *Hagakure-Tai* (Special Attack Unit). Volunteers from the three squadrons filled it. The flight was equipped with Ki-61 *Hien* fighters stripped of excess weight (including armament) to improve high-altitude performance. Pilots were expected to survive the ramming. They were to bail out after the collision, to fly further ramming missions.

These aircraft never attacked F-13s. They were only used against bomber formations. Perhaps this was due to the perception that the F-13s were not attacking Tokyo, while the bomb-laden B-29s were. If so, it was short-sighted. Without the intelligence provided by F-13s, the Twentieth Air Force's bombing effectiveness would have been sharply reduced.

The recon flights provided critical photo-intelligence about Tokyo industries, the transportation network, and defenses. They ripped away the secrecy shrouding Tokyo, even prior to the war. The Twentieth Air Force could not bomb aircraft factories in Tokyo unless they knew where those factories were and what they looked like. Before *Tokyo Rose's* November 1 flight, no one knew where any of Tokyo's strategic targets were located.

By November 11, General Hansell believed he had identified the most important aircraft factories in and near Tokyo, and knew the naval and harbor installations around Tokyo Bay, from Tokyo to Yokosuka. He believed it was time to open the offensive against Japan. The first target would be Tokyo.

The choice was not *in* Tokyo. For their first mission against Tokyo, XXI Bomber Command targeteers selected the Musashino aircraft engine assembly plant. It built engines for the Imperial Army and was next to the Tama aircraft engine factory, which built engines for the Imperial Navy. Both plants were owned by Nakajima. Army Air Force planners estimated these two plants produced 30 to 40 percent of the aircraft engines used in Japan's warplanes. In reality, it was 27 percent. That still made it an excellent target. The Musashino-Tama factories, initially independent, were merged into the Musashi plant. It was west of Ogikubo, outside Tokyo's corporate limits.

The F-13A "Tokyo Rose" aircraft conducted a half-hour photoreconnaissance flight over Tokyo on November 1, 1945. It was two days after it arrived at Saipan, but the crew opted to go despite their fatigue. It was the first US aircraft to fly over Tokyo since the Doolittle Raid in April 1942. (USAF)

Hansell did not want to make the first attack with less than 100 bombers. His intelligence officers estimated they would face 400 to 500 fighters defending just Tokyo. (In reality, in November 1944 Japan had only 375 fighters stationed in the Home Islands.) One hundred bombers was seen as the minimum necessary to provide the defensive fire to survive that onslaught. The first B-29 arrived at Saipan on October 12, 1944, with a slow build-up after then. By November 15, the 73rd Bombardment Wing had 90. Hansell scheduled the first Tokyo mission for November 17, when he felt he would reach his magic number.

The mission, code-named *San Antonio I*, envisioned a daytime strike; visual bombing at 30,000ft by ten to 12 squadrons with nine to 11 B-29s. Each plane would carry ten 500lb bombs, seven general purpose and three incendiary. (These used the AN-M64 casing, but were filled with a mixture of magnesium and jelled gasoline.) To disperse enemy fighters, a

First raid on the Musashino aircraft engine factory

On November 24, 1944, the Twentieth Air Force made its first attack on Tokyo, attacking Nakajima's Aircraft Engine Factory at Musashino. While 110 73rd Bombardment Wing aircraft departed Saipan, by the time the bombers reached the Mount Fuji landmark and turned to head to Musashino, only 87 were left. The rest had aborted or attacked secondary targets.

The Japanese reaction was furious. Every available 10th Air Division fighter was sent to intercept the B-29s. However, the attacks were made in an uncoordinated fashion. Japanese fighters were given the range and heading of the US formation on take-off. They had to seek them out without further guidance once airborne. Thus, they attacked the bomber formation in small groups upon spotting them. This illustration shows an attack occurring early in the air battle, before the B-29s reached Musashino.

Leading the B-29s was *Dauntless Dotty*, a plane commanded by Major Robert K. Morgan, who once commanded the B-17 *Memphis Belle*. He was in the co-pilot's seat, while Brigadier General Emmett "Rosie" O'Donnell, Jr., commander of the 73rd Bombardment Wing, sat in the pilot's seat. The aircraft is at 30,000ft, flying east-northeast. At the instant shown in the plate, it is being attacked by three Japanese aircraft, who are concentrating on the formation's lead aircraft.

A Nakajima Ki-84 *Hayate* has just completed an overhead attack. It dived almost straight down on *Dauntless Dotty*, starting from ahead and 3,000ft above the bomber. While the maneuver minimizes the opportunity of being hit by defensive fire, it provides little time to aim and fire. Meanwhile, two Kawasaki Ki-61 *Hien* are approaching *Dauntless Dotty* from head-on and just below the bomber. Only the two .50cal machine guns of the B-29's lower forward turret can reach the oncoming enemy aircraft. With a closing speed of 600+ mph, it offers little time to aim and fire.

Nakajima's Musashi aircraft engine factory at Musashino. This reconnaissance photo of the plant was taken prior to the first raid on it. The plant was subject to over a dozen air raids by B-29s and US Navy warplanes over the course of the campaign. It was the most frequently raided place in Tokyo. (LOC)

diversionary "raid" on Nagoya was to run concurrently. In reality, it would be conducted by F-13s dropping chaff to spoof the radar return of a large bomber formation. The XXI Bomber Command planned to coordinate the attack with the US Navy's Third Fleet. The B-29 raid would attack simultaneously with a carrier strike against Tokyo.

The plan quickly fell apart. The Navy, preoccupied supporting the Leyte invasion in the Philippines, had backed out. Then the launch date got washed out, literally. Unusual winds from the east meant the aircraft had to make an uphill take-off run from Saipan. That combined with heavy rains forced a weather scrub to November 18. More rain followed. Not until the morning of November 24 did the winds shift back to normal and the skies dawned clear. At 0615hrs on Saipan, the first B-29 took flight on the Twentieth Air Force's first combat mission to Japan. Target: Tokyo.

The first aircraft aloft was a B-29 named *Dauntless Dotty*. At the controls was the commander of the 73rd Bombardment Wing, Brigadier General Emmett "Rosie" O'Donnell, Jr., a veteran of combat in the Philippines in 1941–42. In the co-pilot's seat was *Dauntless Dotty*'s commander, Major Robert K. Morgan, once command pilot of the B-17 *Memphis Belle* in Europe. One hundred and ten B-29s followed *Dauntless Dotty* into the sky.

The F-13s followed. Instead of going to Nagoya, they too were headed to Tokyo. Approaching from a different direction, they dropped chaff, hoping to draw fighters away from the bombers. Following that, they were to do post-strike photography of Musashi to permit bomb damage assessment.

Almost nothing went right. Seventeen B-29s aborted before reaching Japan. Six others which reached Tokyo were unable to drop their bombs due to mechanical failure. Weather was uncooperative. Clouds between the ground and the B-29s obscured the target. The high-flying B-29s were caught in a 120mph tailwind. This pushed the bombers over their aim points at 450mph, too fast for accuracy. Crosswinds scattered the bombs dropped.

Only 24 bombers attacked Musashi. Their accuracy was dismal. Only 48 of the 240 bombs dropped landed in the factory area. Three of those were duds. The 500lb general purpose bombs proved too light to cause serious damage to the reinforced concrete of the main factory buildings. The fires set by the incendiaries were quickly quenched by the factory's *bogodan*. Postwar assessment indicated the bombs only damaged 2.4 percent of the machinery at Musashino and just 1 percent of its buildings. Worker casualties totaled 57 dead and 75 wounded.

The rest of the strike force, 64 bombers, was clouded out. These switched to secondary targets in Tokyo's urban area and dockyards. Thirty-five of those 64 aircraft bombed using radar because their targets were cloud covered. Damage was minimal.

Japanese reaction was not. The 10th Flying Division sent every fighter available airborne, including night fighters. After consolidating crew reports post-flight, Twentieth Air Force intelligence estimated 125 Japanese aircraft had intercepted the bombers. Since the 10th Flying Division had only 90 fighters, and some were unserviceable, this was due to double-counting or triple-counting attacking aircraft. The Japanese made uncoordinated attacks in flight, and some aircraft made multiple passes at the B-29s. The exaggeration was understandable.

Nor were the Japanese successful. Flak failed to damage the bombers. Only one B-29 was brought down by enemy action. It was rammed by a damaged *Shoki*, which ripped the Superfortress's starboard horizontal stabilizer off. The *Shoki* was not a *Hagakure-Tai* aircraft. Rather, the pilot feared his fighter would not make it to base and decided to take a B-29 with him.

The bomber splashed into the Pacific 20 miles east of the coast, killing all aboard. The only other aircraft lost ran out of fuel returning to Saipan. Its crew was saved. Eleven other B-29s returned with bullet or cannon damage; eight from enemy fighter fire. Three others were hit by overeager B-29 gunners. In all, the 73rd Wing had one man killed, four injured, and 11 missing, presumed dead.

In turn, B-29 gunners claimed to have shot down seven Japanese fighters, probably downed 18 others, and damaged nine. Those claims were as exaggerated as the Japanese fighter numbers, with plenty of double- and triple-counting of claims. In reality, B-29 gunners had downed five fighters and damaged nine others.

The post-mission damage assessment was frustrated by weather. When the F-13s arrived, the ground was almost completely obscured. Strike photos showed only 16 bomb bursts in the target area. Clouds hid the rest. What was clear was Musashi was still in business, turning out aircraft engines.

The raid set the pattern for the next three months – for both sides. Neither side could seriously hurt the other. US bombing was inaccurate. Japanese resistance was ineffective. Unescorted B-29s could survive over Tokyo. Mechanical problems and fuel management proved a bigger risk to B-29 survival than Japanese fighters or antiaircraft.

The Twentieth Air Force returned to Tokyo on November 27. Although the 73rd Wing had 119 B-29s, only 87 were operational. Six of these experienced issues prior to take-off, and only 81 Superfortresses headed to Japan that day. The target was Musashi once more. Once again, weather interfered with bombing. Musashi was completely clouded over. Most bombed the secondary target, Tokyo's docks, using radar bombing. Others bombed tertiary targets south of Tokyo: Hamamatsu, Numazu, Shizuoka, and Osaka. One B-29 and its crew were lost as they ditched returning to base.

Two days later, the B-29s returned to Tokyo. Since the weather was forecast to be bad, Hansell decided to try a high-altitude night mission, depending on radar for targeting. Only 30 B-29s were sent, striking Tokyo's docks and industrial areas. They dropped a mixture of general purpose and incendiary bombs using AN/APQ-13 radar. It was good enough to determine the outline of a coast, but could not pick out individual factories, even large ones. Results were negligible, but so were losses. Antiaircraft and night fighters proved equally ineffective and all 30 bombers returned safely.

The Nakajima aircraft factory at Ota was the next target. In the Kantō Plain, it was 40 miles northwest of Tokyo in Gunma Prefecture. A maximum effort was planned for 3 December, but weather forecasts were bad; clouds covering the target and 180mph winds over the target. Planners shifted the target to Musashi once more.

This time the skies were clear. Eighty-six bombers took off for Tokyo; 76 reached the city; 59 bombed the target. Winds scattered the bombs. Of nearly 600 bombs dropped, only 26 landed within the footprint of the Musashino plant. Strike photography showed the damage done was trivial. The 500lb bombs used caused minor damage to buildings, but almost none to machinery.

The Japanese fighters proved moderately successful this mission. Six B-29s failed to return and six were damaged. Three B-29s were downed by ramming. (A fourth ramming attempt damaged its target, but the bomber successfully returned to the Marianas.) Two were shot down over Japan by gunfire. The Japanese claimed five B-29s shot down, and lost six aircraft.

APPROXIMATE SCALE IN FEET
50 150
0 100 200 400 600 800

The results of the first raid on Musashino are shown in this post-mission photograph. The damage that resulted was trivial. Postwar analysis rated the damage as "negligible." Only 24 B-29s bombed the target and only 16 bombs landed within the factory complex. Fifty-seven workers were killed and 75 wounded. (LOC)

Tokyo received a three-week respite, as the Twentieth Air Force turned its attention to Iwo Jima and Nagoya. Finally, on December 27, Hansell returned to Tokyo. The Musashino complex of the Musashi plant was once more the target. Results were as dismal as those of the previous raids. Seventy-two aircraft were sent; only 39 reached and bombed the target. Only 26 500lb bombs landed within the complex, doing little damage. Some of the strays set fire to a hospital, giving the Japanese a propaganda coup.

Japanese fighters were waiting for the B-29s, Imperial Navy aircraft joining in on the attack. The fighters swept in, attacking as the bombers were making their bomb run. One B-29, named *Uncle Tom's Cabin* was rammed by two *Hagakure-Tai Hiens*. This did not bring the bomber down, but damaged it enough that it fell out of formation. It was swarmed by the Japanese fighters and shot down over Tokyo Bay.

Two other B-29s failed to return. One crashed shortly after take-off; a second was forced to ditch returning to Saipan. The Japanese claimed five B-29s shot down, five probably shot down, and 25 damaged. US claims were equally exaggerated. At least nine Japanese fighters were claimed to have been shot down by *Uncle Tom's Cabin* alone. In reality, Japan lost six, two Imperial Army fighters expended by ramming and four others shot down by B-29 gunners.

Tokyo got another two-week rest following that. The 73rd Wing returned on January 9, 1945. Once more the target was Musashino, and once more the results were the same. Hansell sent 72 B-29s. Jet-stream tore the formation apart as the bombers were on final approach. Only 18 B-29s bombed the target. Again the winds scattered the bombs. Just 25 bombs fell within the plant footprint. One warehouse was destroyed; two others damaged.

The 10th Flying Division and Imperial Navy's 302nd Kotai took advantage of the opportunity offered by the bombers, flying in scattered formations of three to nine aircraft. Six bombers went down. Four were rammed by Imperial Army fighters, one shot down by an Imperial Army fighter, and another by a Navy aircraft. Another six returned to base shot up. Most of the lost or damaged B-29s belonged to the group that reached Musashino.

Frustration, faltering, and the Navy's in: January 27 to March 4, 1945

B-29s of the 73rd Wing attacked Tokyo six times in as many weeks with negligible results. The focus of five of those attacks, the Musashino factory in the Musashi aircraft engine complex was largely undamaged. Nor had they done much better elsewhere in Japan. The damage done failed to exceed the expenditure in fuel, bombs, and bullets used during those missions. Add in the aircraft and lives lost, even with the relatively light losses, and the net return was negative. In the United States, when a sports team does badly, the team's owner replaces the coach.

General Henry "Hap" Arnold commanded the Army Air Force. He "owned" the Twentieth Air Force, which reported directly to him. Hansell took command of XXI Bomber Command on August 28, 1944, arrived at Saipan on October 12, and began combat operations against Japan on November 27. Throughout, he remained stubbornly committed to high-altitude precision bomber.

Despite Arnold's directive to attempt a maximum effort nighttime incendiary attack, Hansell's 30-plane raid to Tokyo was the only night incendiary raid he attempted at Tokyo. It was a half-hearted effort, hardly the maximum effort raid envisioned by Arnold. The only other incendiary raid Hansell attempted was a high-altitude daylight raid on Nagoya. Only 57 aircraft reached the city. The fires started were easily contained by Nagoya's efficient fire department.

Hansell also rejected requests to use B-29s to drop mines in Japanese coastal waters. He claimed the effort would take away from the strategic bombing campaign. The claim had merit when the 73rd was the only B-29 wing at Saipan. When the 313th Wing arrived on December 27, 1944, Hansell had them train in minelaying against the day he had enough aircraft to bomb and drop mines. Even then he did not view minelaying as part of a strategic air campaign.

Arnold felt Hansell lacked the flexibility to turn the B-29 into a war-winning weapon. Arnold was probably right. Brigadier General Curtis LeMay had taken over the faltering XX Bomber Command, operating B-29s in China and India and turned the outfit around. LeMay willingly experimented with any tactic that made B-29s more effective: daylight high-altitude *and* medium-level precision bombing, nighttime precision bombing, minelaying, and area incendiary raids. His aircraft made a highly successful fire raid against Hankow in December 1944.

Early in January, Arnold decided to replace Hansell with LeMay. The decision was probably made around New Year's Day. Since LeMay was in India, he did not formally relieve Hansell until January 20, 1945.

Ironically, Hansell finally succeeded with a high-altitude precision attack the day before he was relieved. He sent 77 bombers against the Kawasaki aircraft factory in Akashi. The attack was made 5,000ft lower than previously, with bombs dropped at 24,500ft to 27,500ft, in clear skies. Fighter opposition was light (the target was isolated from major urban areas). Bombing accuracy was excellent and the plant was smashed. Aircraft production dropped 90 percent.

Nothing changed at first with LeMay in command. His first two missions, against Nagoya and Tokyo were re-runs of Hansell's missions, especially the Tokyo raid. Flown January 27, it was the first attack on Tokyo in over two weeks. The target was Musashino. LeMay sent 76 bombers to Tokyo, but twelve returned to base before reaching Japan. The 64 that arrived encountered high winds, a hot reception from fighters, and a target hidden under a layer of clouds.

The Japanese fighter counterattack was furious. Ten Japanese fighters rammed B-29s, although five of the rammed bombers apparently returned to the Marianas. (One broke in half after landing, although the crew survived.) Four others were shot down by Imperial Army

Haywood Hansell strikes a pose in front of a map of Tokyo and Tokyo Bay while in command of the XXI Bomber Command. He was a resolute believer in strategic bombing, especially precision bombing. His tactical inflexibility and inability to deliver meaningful results led to his relief in January 1945. (AC)

and Navy night fighters acting as daylight interceptors. These carried enough heavy guns to reliably down a B-29. (Two attacked from below, using upward firing guns.) One other B-29 was shot down by a single-engine fighter, likely a *Shoki*. In all, the 73rd Wing lost nine B-29s, and ten damaged.

The bombers got their licks in, downing 16 aircraft. Losses were especially heavy against the twin engine fighters. At least four were shot down by Japanese records, with a fifth making a successful forced landing at its airfield. (One *Hien* also managed a forced landing after ramming a B-29.) The US claimed 60 fighter kills, 17 probables, and 39 damaged, roughly the total number of Japanese fighters available to defend Tokyo. Japanese claims were nearly as exaggerated: 22 B-29s shot down. Even with the actual losses on both sides, it was the bloodiest battle in terms of aircraft losses to date in the Tokyo campaign.

That raid ended the first phase of the US campaign against Tokyo. LeMay decided to attack easier targets than Tokyo and Nagoya. He felt those two cities, Tokyo particularly, were too hard to crack with one B-29 wing. The 313th Wing had begun arriving in late December and he wanted to train them up – and improve the training of the 73rd Wing – before returning to Tokyo. (The 313th would be joined by the 314th in early March, the 58th – relocated from China – in May and the 315th in June. All required training before being committed to combat.) The Twentieth Air Force did not return to Tokyo until February 19.

That did not mean Tokyo took a break during that period. On February 10, the Twentieth Air Force flew over Tokyo to reach Ota, a further target. Between February 16 and 17, the US Navy came for a visit, launching two days of airstrikes on the Kantō Plain, including Tokyo.

The Ota raid was the second multi-wing strike by the Twentieth Air Force, with aircraft from both the 73rd and 313th Wings. A total of 118 B-29s left the Marianas, but ten turned back before reaching Japan. Eighty-four others headed to Ota, while 14 went after secondary targets. The primary target was Ota's Nakajima aircraft factory. It produced Ki-84s, one of the Imperial Army's best fighters. It hit a maximum production of 300 *Hayate* in December 1944. By February, parts shortages reduced output to 100 aircraft per month. It remained an important target.

Ota was 40 miles northwest of Tokyo, in neighboring Gunma Prefecture, but the path to it was within Tokyo's air defense region. The path the B-29s took to reach it passed near Tokyo. Both the Army's 10th Flying Division, and the Navy's 71st Air Flotilla, scrambled fighters to engage the bombers. Both sent everything they had: 90 Imperial Army aircraft and over 300 Imperial Navy fighters.

Major General Curtis LeMay (left), Brigadier General Haywood Hansell (center), and Brigadier General Roger Ramey at Saipan on January 7, 1945. LeMay had instructions to consult with Hansell when he arrived. He was ordered to relieve Hansell a week later and did so on January 18. Ramey, deputy commander at Saipan, replaced LeMay as commander of the XX Bomber Command. (AC)

This was not as formidable as it appeared on paper. The Army total included night fighters and *Hiens*. Perhaps half were the formidable *Shoki*. While 74 fighters from the Navy's 302nd Group were *Raiden*, 240 from the 252nd Group were Zeroes, poor performers at B-29 altitudes. Moreover, it was a new unit. Most of its pilots were green, still in training.

A massive aerial brawl erupted over the Kantō Plain. The 70th Group of the 10th Flying Division caught up with the US bomber formations as they were on final approach to the target. In a series of furious encounters, four Imperial Army fighters rammed B-29s, while two B-29s collided over the target, bringing both down. Five B-29s went down over Japan; seven others ditched on the way home due to battle damage. Twenty-nine other B-29s were damaged. The Japanese claimed 21 shot down and lost nine fighters.

The raid paid off for the US. Eighty percent of the bombload was 500lb general purpose bombs; 20 percent incendiaries. The weather was clear. Despite that, only one-eighth of

In response to a daytime Twentieth Air Force attack on Tokyo on January 27, the Imperial Japanese Army and Navy put every fighter they had airborne. This included using twin-engine night fighters, like this Gekkō during this daylight raid. Due to their heavy batteries, night fighters shot down four B-29s on that day. (AC)

The US Navy comes calling

On February 16–17, 1945, the US Navy's Task Force 58 conducted two days of airstrikes on Tokyo and its environs. One of the targets hit on February 16 was the largely undamaged Musashino aircraft engine factory. The Army Air Force had attempted to destroy it on six previous missions, but only slightly damaged it. This plate shows the attack by the US Navy at its climax, in the early afternoon of February 16.

The factory was attacked by 73 US Navy aircraft from three different carriers: 33 Hellcats, 30 Avengers, and ten Helldivers. There was no Japanese fighter opposition. The Navy opened the day by attacking Japanese airfields, and by noon, there were few Japanese in the air and none around Musashino. The Navy could work the place over at its leisure.

The illustration shows how the US Navy attacked a ground installation in 1945 when it had local air superiority. Sixteen Hellcats, ten Helldivers, and nine Avengers can be seen. Eight Hellcats are flying top cover in two flights of four, to intercept any enemy fighters attempting to attack the bombers. Eight other Hellcats are low, strafing antiaircraft positions around the factory. This suppressive fire permits the bombers to attack unmolested.

The ten Helldivers are targeting the main assembly building, a three-story reinforced-concrete structure. The lead Helldiver on each flight has pushed over for a dive-bombing attack. The remaining four are following, with the second aircraft beginning its pushover. Meanwhile, nine Avengers are conducting level-bombing attacks on the warehouses and machine shop buildings on the east side of the factory complex. They will be followed by two more waves of Avengers which will follow up, attacking buildings undamaged earlier.

The whole raid lasted just under an hour. During two days of bombing, the US Navy planted over 100 bombs on buildings in the factory complex. This attack planted 39 tons of bombs on Musashino, destroying ten buildings and damaging 20 others.

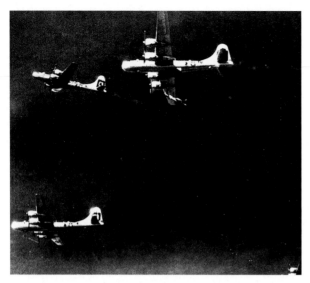

Ten Japanese fighters rammed B-29s that attacked Tokyo on January 27. This photo shows the result of a collision between a B-29 and a Japanese fighter. This is not a *Hien* from the 244th Sendai, but appears to be a twin-engine fighter. The pilot chose to ram due to damage to his aircraft. (NMAF)

the bombs dropped landed within the plant. Half of the 500lb bombs were duds, but seven incendiaries and 51 general purpose bombs detonated. They caused heavy damage to the plant. The incendiaries caused fires that destroyed five wooden buildings; six metal buildings were heavily damaged by exploding AN-M64s. Seventy-four *Hayates* were destroyed on the assembly line, while dozens of fuselage, wing, and tail assemblies were also destroyed. Production was reduced by two-thirds through loss of buildings and machinery.

Six days later, it was Tokyo's turn. The visitors were not the Twentieth Air Force; they were Task Force 58 of the US Navy, the first attack on Tokyo by carrier-based aircraft since the Doolittle Raid.

The US Navy finished a highly successful 28-day carrier raid into the South China Sea in January. They wanted a further demonstration of their ability to strike Imperial Japan. Admirals Chester Nimitz, commanding the US Pacific Fleet and Raymond Spruance, commanding the Fifth Fleet and its attached Task Force 58 (the Fast Carrier Force), felt Tokyo was a good place to start.

The stated reason for the attack was to draw Japanese attention away from the planned invasion of Iwo Jima, scheduled for February 19. The main and unstated reason was to show the Navy was as capable of being used to project strategic air power as the Army Air Force. One target on the Navy's list was the Musashino aircraft engine plant. If they could succeed in damaging it where the Army Air Force had failed, the raid would be a success.

On February 10, when the Fast Carrier Force left its Ulithi anchorage, it had 16 fast carriers: nine Essex-class fleet carriers, two prewar fleet carriers (*Enterprise* and *Saratoga*), and five light carriers. Aboard were over 1,200 warplanes: 840 fighters, 240 torpedo bombers, and 135 dive bombers. Roughly 170 of these were radar-equipped, capable of all-weather operations. The fighters could carry bombs. Except for fighter sweeps, half were outfitted as fighter bombers to strike ground targets. This formidable force vastly outnumbered the aircraft assigned to defend Tokyo.

The Fast Carrier Force took a roundabout approach to Honshu, sailing well east of the Bonin Islands. The route was scouted by F-13s and US Navy PBY Liberators to ensure no Japanese picket craft were present. After five days, it reached the run-in point, 600nmi southeast of Honshu. TF58 refueled three times along the way. At 0800hrs on February 15, the destroyers were topped off at the run-in point. From there, they steamed at 25 knots to arrive at their launch point, 60 miles from the Honshu coast and 125 miles from Tokyo. Due to overcast weather, the carriers reached that spot undetected.

Launch operations started at 0600hrs on February 16. Flying conditions were bad, a 4,000ft ceiling with broken clouds at 1,000ft and intermittent rain and snow squalls, with a moderate gale from the northeast. Despite that, no one wanted to turn around. The first aircraft off conducted a series of massive fighter sweeps, intended to clear the skies for the bombers. These went to the airfields known to be in the area. The first one was met by 100 Japanese aircraft. Forty were shot down in the ensuing melee; they were probably from the green 252nd Group.

Fighters finding no aircraft in the air strafed Japanese airfields throughout the Kantō Plain. Shifts of Corsairs and Hellcats kept the major airfields covered throughout the rest of the day.

The weather cleared temporarily around 1030hrs. The scheduled fighter sweeps were still occurring when Admiral Marc Mitscher, commanding the Fast Carrier Force, ordered the bombers out. He was afraid the weather would worsen in the afternoon. By 1130hrs, the first bomber strikes were launching. Their targets the first day were the Nakajima aircraft factories in Ota, nearby Koizumi, and the Nakajima aircraft engine factory at Musashi. All three factories took damage.

Musashi was attacked by 73 US Navy aircraft from three different carriers: 33 Hellcats, 30 Avengers, and ten Helldivers. They dropped 67,750lb of bombs on the buildings, causing serious damage. It suffered more damage from that raid than from the accumulated B-29 raids to that date. The damage had Nakajima management considering closing the factory.

Sunset brought no respite to the Japanese airfields. US Navy night fighters and bombers kept them covered throughout the night. For years, the US Navy had suffered nighttime counterattacks from the Japanese after launching strikes at Japanese bases. This time, TF58 spent the night undisturbed while cruising off Honshu's coast.

The airstrikes resumed the next morning, with aircraft launching before dawn. Scouts hunted down shipping in and around Tokyo Bay. These were followed by fighter sweeps, and then bombers. Musashino was revisited, along with the adjacent Tama plant. They also attacked the Showa Aircraft Company plant at Tachikawa. Other bombers struck the harbor area, sinking several ships, including the 10,600-ton cargo liner *Yamashita Maru*. Several small patrol craft were damaged.

Mitscher shut down the attacks at 1130hrs on February 17 due to bad weather. Thereafter, TF58 turned towards Iwo Jima to support the invasion scheduled for February 19. The Fast Carrier Force lost 60 aircraft to combat and 28 to operational accidents. It claimed 341 aircraft shot down and another 125 destroyed on the ground. Actual Japanese losses were probably lower, but they were substantial. The Imperial Navy's 252nd Fighter Group played no further role in Tokyo's defense. Presumably, it took enough casualties to remove it from the order of battle.

LeMay tried two more high-altitude precision attacks against Musashi; one on February 19 and a final one on March 4. Both were massive two-wing raids. The February 19 raid saw 172 B-29s strike Musashi, while the March 4 raid had 192. Both achieved identical results: no damage to the engine plant. In both cases, rain and clouds covered the factory. The bombers

A formation of Avengers from the Essex-class carrier *Bunker Hill* flies over the Kantō Plain on February 16, 1945. The US Navy struck a wide assortment of airfields and factories during two days of airstrikes on the Home Islands. The US Navy strikes hurt the Tokyo area more than all Twentieth Air Force raids to that date. (AC)

hit secondary targets, the port and urban areas near the coast of Tokyo Bay. The damage done to these areas was insignificant, and several B-29s were lost. High-altitude precision bombing had proved a failure, at least at Tokyo. As March 1945 began, Tokyo was winning its battle against the Twentieth Air Force.

The first fire raid: March 9–10, 1945

The Army Air Force headquarters in Washington, D.C. prodded Hansell and was prodding LeMay to test incendiary attacks. Hansell was fully committed to winning a strategic air war through high-altitude strategic bombing. Hansell's foot-dragging on fire raids was one reason for his relief. LeMay was more open to it. LeMay was committed simply to winning a strategic air war. He did not care what missions it took to achieve victory. After eight unsuccessful efforts to destroy Musashi through high-altitude precision bombing, LeMay was willing to try something different.

On February 25, LeMay conducted a test of incendiary area bombing. He sent out 231 B-29s. These included aircraft from three wings, the 73rd, the 313th, and the newly arrived 314th. The 314th was so new, only one-third of its authorized strength was operational, and those crews were still undergoing shakedown training. Each aircraft carried 5,000lb of bombs, one 500lb general purpose bomb, with the balance made up of M69 incendiaries in 500lb bundles.

Only 201 aircraft arrived at Japan, with 30 aircraft aborting shortly after take-off. Of the 201, 172 found the target. They dropped 453.7 tons of bombs on Tokyo. The results were spectacular. One square mile of Tokyo was burned out; 27,970 buildings were destroyed or burned out. Casualties numbered in the thousands. US losses were minimal.

The raid made LeMay believe in the effectiveness of area bombing using the B-29. He made one more high-altitude precision strike, the March 4 attack on Musashi described earlier. On March 6, he observed: "This outfit has been getting a lot of publicity without having really accomplished a hell of a lot in bombing results." To fix that, he planned a strike

of unprecedented size and fury. He stood down his fleet for five days. The pause allowed Twentieth Air Force mechanics to fix battle damage, perform maintenance, and overhaul engines and check systems on all aircraft. It allowed a raid of unprecedented size, using every available aircraft.

Not just the size of the raid was unprecedented. So were the tactics. LeMay realized success lay in the mass of his attack. The Tokyo and Nagoya fire raids launched by Hansell were contained due to the relatively few incendiaries dropped. The February 25 raid was more successful, but burning out Tokyo one square mile at a time would take over two years of daily raids. Damage had to be done on a larger scale.

A B-29 of the 314th Bombardment Wing sets down on a runway in Guam. The 314th was one of the three wings used on the first Tokyo fire raid. To ensure the largest possible strike, LeMay had a five-day mission stand down to commit the maximum number of aircraft to the strike. (NMAF)

Bombardier's view: the first fire raid

The Twentieth Air Force incendiary attack on Tokyo made on March 9–10, 1945 was the first maximum effort incendiary attack on Japan. It was also the deadliest, due to it triggering a wave firestorm. It was also considered a risky mission by the crews flying it. The planes were to come in low and individually. This illustration shows the attack as it would be viewed from the bombardier's position.

It shows an aircraft approaching the drop point. It is still early in the raid, after the pathfinders have finished but before most of the main body arrives. The time is about 0230hrs. The airplane is flying east-southeast over northern Tokyo. The Sumida River can be seen through the nose. So can the fires that have started and are spreading. The airplane is at 8,000ft, low enough that the crew compartment does not need to be pressurized and the crew does not need oxygen.

The target area is Tokyo's Asakusa Ward. This is Tokyo's most crowded neighborhood, filled with cramped wooden buildings lining narrow, crooked alleys. It is perfect tinder for incendiaries. Fires can be seen on both sides of the Sumida River, as some earlier B-29s dropped their incendiaries late. The fires are spreading and beginning to merge. Smoke is beginning to obscure the target area, but flames can be seen beneath the smoke, providing an aiming point.

Now it is this aircraft's turn. The aircraft is carrying a load of M-64 incendiaries. The bombardier could use the Norden bombsight seen directly under the center pane of the nose glass, but precision is unimportant on this night. All he has to do is drop the bombs so they fall on a part of the city not already on fire. Once the incendiaries are gone, they can head home.

Armorers load incendiary clusters into the bomb bay of a B-29 in preparation for the Tokyo fire raid of March 9–10. Only incendiaries were carried during this mission. The majority of the aircraft participating in the raid carried clusters of M-69s, like the one shown here. (AC)

He planned a night strike, with aircraft proceeding to the target individually. That eliminated fuel needed to move into and stay in formation. He also planned to attack from an unprecedentedly low altitude. Aircraft would bomb at altitudes between 5,000 and 8,000ft. No fuel would be required to climb to 30,000ft, with bombs substituted for fuel. He planned to save more weight by not carrying any ammunition for defensive guns and leaving the gunners in the Marianas. Eliminating the ammunition reduced weight another 3,200lb. Total weight savings from ammunition and gasoline meant the bombers could carry over 13,000lb of bombs, instead of 5,000lb.

Aircrew reaction to the plans was mixed. Crews liked the size of the raid, believing numbers offered safety. They appreciated attacking under cover of darkness. But most believed attacking at such low altitudes would be suicidal. They felt Japanese antiaircraft would tear them apart flying that low. The idea of going in without ammunition horrified them. Crews reacted extremely badly to leaving the gunners on the ground. They were a team, becoming a family after flying combat missions together. The gunners resented being left behind. The rest of the crew felt part of them was being left behind.

Concerns about the negative impact on crew morale convinced LeMay to modify his plans. The gunners would accompany the flight as normal. Further, LeMay decided to arm the bottom turrets. However, the only thing they were supposed to fire at was Japanese searchlights on the ground. They were not to fire at anything else. LeMay worried more about B-29s being damaged by friendly fire from other B-29s than of the damage they might suffer from night fighters.

That was the only change. LeMay viewed the night fighter threat as insignificant. He was aware of the low number of Japanese night fighters and their poor quality. He believed the flak risk was acceptable. Japanese light antiaircraft artillery was ineffective at altitudes higher than 4,000ft. Its heavy antiaircraft artillery reached peak effectiveness at altitudes between 15,000ft and 28,000ft. There was less time to track targets the lower the aircraft flew. At night, Japanese antiaircraft guns were dependent on searchlights and radar for target acquisition. Japanese gun-laying radar worked poorly.

LeMay counted on the element of surprise. Prior to Iwo Jima's capture, it served as an early warning location. Its occupation eliminated the Bonins as an early warning location. Hachijō-Jima was now the most distant radar station. The lower altitude also meant search radar would detect the bombers closer than usual.

Japanese radar did not return altitude information. It was possible radar operators might realize the closer initial appearance of incoming aircraft was due to them flying at a lower altitude than usual, but only experienced operators would grasp its significance. LeMay bet the radar operators lacked that sophistication and had no way of relaying the information if they did. He believed the Japanese would expect the bombers to approach at 30,000ft. They would pre-position night fighters at that altitude and fuse antiaircraft artillery shells to explode at that altitude. If so, only a direct hit would bring down a Superfortress. Otherwise, the shells would explode tens of thousands of feet above the bomber stream.

At 1817hrs on March 9, 1945, shortly before sunset, B-29s began to lift off Marianas runways. The 73rd Bombardment Wing left Saipan, the 313th Tinian, and the 314th from Guam. The 313th, having a longer distance, took off 40 minutes earlier than the wings based in Saipan and Tinian to permit a simultaneous arrival over Tokyo. After two-and-three-quarter hours, 325 Superfortresses were in the air, heading to Tokyo seven hours away.

LeMay put his best radar operators in the lead B-29s, to serve as pathfinders. They were to use radar navigation to reach that night's intended target, in and around Tokyo's Asakusa district, five miles northeast of the Imperial Palace. It was the most heavily built-up section of Tokyo, a warren of narrow alleys and densely packed wood-frame buildings. Most held both residences and home factories. The Tokyo average population density in its urban area was 103,000 inhabitants per square mile. In Asakusa it was 135,000. The pathfinders were to mark the aiming point. Aircraft following were to drop their bombs next to any fire they saw burning.

The pathfinder aircraft each carried 184 70lb M47 bombs, clustered six to a bomb station; a total weight of 20,880lb. The clusters were set to fall apart at a 100ft altitude, high enough to scatter each cluster across a city block. Each M47 had the capability to start a fire large enough to require a firetruck to respond. One squadron from each wing, 12 aircraft, served as pathfinders. The rest of the B-29s carried 24 500lb clusters of M-69 incendiaries. These fell apart into smaller clusters at 2,000ft at 50ft intervals, scattering widely as they fell.

Although the bombers encountered heavy clouds traveling to Tokyo, weather over Tokyo was clearer than usual. The initial aircraft found only one-tenth to three-tenths cloud cover over the city. The aiming point was easily identified by the pathfinders. Shortly after midnight in Tokyo, they began marking their target with M-47 bombs.

Small home factories filled the Asakusa Ward. They employed one to five workers and made subassemblies and parts critical to Japan's war effort. They were particularly hard hit during the fire raid. Housed in inflammable wooden structures, ruined machinery and ashes were all that remained after fire swept through them. (LOC)

Soon, the Asakusa was ablaze. The M-47s scattered, creating several thousand individual fires. A 13mph wind was blowing when the raid started. The fires quickly merged together. Even before the last pathfinder finished, Tokyo's fire department had mobilized all fire trucks in the immediate area, and were calling in reserves from more distant stations. Even so, there were already too many fires to deal with.

Things got worse during the night. Follow-on aircraft dropped loads of M-69s on unburning parts of Tokyo adjacent to the fire. Tokyo was marked with a massive red glow that even the worst navigator could spot. Cloud cover increased as the night went on, but radar navigation and the glow of existing fires guided bombardiers to their targets.

The conflagration grew as the night went on. So did the wind. By 0200hrs, it had increased to 21mph. The winds fed the fires. In turn, fires fed the wind. By 0400hrs, winds had increased to 28mph, near gale force. On the ground, the fires merged into a massive line firestorm. As the fires built, convection forced oxygen from higher, cooler altitudes down to the ground, where it fed further fire growth. At ground level, this phenomenon led to gusts of up to 50mph, storm force winds. Instead of rain, these winds held fire. Normally, a firestorm created a vortex, high into the sky, but high winds prevented that. It formed a wall of fire that swept in a line across Tokyo, incinerating anything in its path. It was so fierce it jumped standard firebreaks. It stopped only after hitting a major obstacle, such as the Arawaka River past the Asakusa's eastern side.

Meanwhile, more B-29s dropped their loads. For nearly three hours, incendiaries fell on Tokyo. By the time the last bombers were approaching Tokyo, the target was almost

The fires set in Tokyo during the predawn hours of March 10 continued burning well after the sun rose on that day. Photoreconnaissance aircraft captured the scope of the destruction in this photograph. Smoke continued rising from the burned-out sections of Tokyo late into the following day. (LOC)

completely obscured by smoke. Despite that, the fires were so fierce the sky was almost as bright as during the day. Tail gunners reported seeing the fire's glow 150 miles from Tokyo on their homeward journey.

The dire predictions of heavy enemy resistance proved false. Night fighters were at, and shells set to, 30,000ft when the pathfinders arrived. They escaped damage from either enemy aircraft or antiaircraft fire. The flak soon adjusted and some of the early aircraft reported moderate to heavy flak. That died away as antiaircraft positions were overrun by flames. Over the course of the night, antiaircraft fire shot down nine B-29s over Tokyo and damaged five others badly enough they were forced down on the way home. Their crews were recovered by air–sea rescue teams at sea. Another 42 B-29s came home with flak damage of varying severity. The worst-damaged put down at Iwo Jima.

As LeMay predicted, the night fighter threat proved almost non-existent. Crews reported only 76 sightings of night fighters, and only 40 attacks. None caused serious damage to bombers. Generally, the only B-29s attacked by night fighters were those coned by searchlights. As with the antiaircraft guns, the searchlight positions were overrun by fires as the night went on. The total B-29 loss rate for the mission was 4.2 percent. While not trivial, it was acceptable, especially set against the damage done. It was lower than the 5.7 percent loss rate for January 1945.

By dawn, the surviving bombers were all over the Pacific heading to base. Tokyo was still burning. It would continue burning until mid-morning on March 10. By the time the fires died down, nearly 16 miles of Tokyo, its most heavily built-up section, was ashes. Wood-and-bamboo dwellings were completely gone. Even "fireproof" reinforced concrete buildings were burned-out shells. The incinerated area included one-fifth of Asakusa's industrial area and two-thirds of its commercial area. It was gone, literally overnight. The industry destroyed was the fraction supplying the rest of Tokyo's industries with parts and assemblies.

Losses were high. One-quarter of Tokyo's buildings, 267,171, were destroyed that night. Tokyo's fire department lost 95 fire engines and 125 firemen. Over 1 million were now homeless. Death estimates ranged from the official count of 83,793 to as high as 135,000. Over 40,000 were injured. This was 20 times higher than any future incendiary raid, even those involving significantly more aircraft.

There were several reasons for the unexpectedly high death toll. The raid took place in one of the most densely populated quarters of Japan. There were relatively few firebreaks. The most important reasons were twofold: the unexpected nature of the raid and the resulting firestorm.

The best way to survive a conventional raid is sheltering in a secure bomb shelter. A close hit can still kill through overpressure, but you are safe from everything else. The best way to survive a fire raid is to evacuate the burning area. This is possible. The fire typically spreads at speeds slower than a walking person.

Residents initially treated the raid as a conventional raid, often sheltering in the basements of fire-resistant concrete buildings. They remained as the fire built up, only attempting evacuation when they were surrounded by flames. By that time, the firestorm had begun, superheating the air and making escape impossible. Death soon followed.

Aircraft factory raids: April 1–12, 1945

The Twentieth Air Force left Tokyo alone for the rest of March. It focused on other cities. In those nine days that followed the first Tokyo fire raid, the Twentieth Air Force conducted a fire-bombing tour. They hit three other major cities with incendiary raids between March 11 and March 19: Nagoya, Osaka, and Kobe. Nagoya was hit twice, once immediately after the Tokyo raid and once at the end of the cycle. All four raids were devastating, although results were not as spectacular as the first Tokyo strike. Osaka and Kobe each had over 8 square

An old man and a child await evacuation amid their baggage. The March fire raid left 1 million Tokyo residents homeless. In the wake of it, prefecture officials accelerated evacuation of non-essential residents. The elderly and children received priority for evacuation. Evacuees were those leaving voluntarily. Departure was subsidized, but they had to find their own lodgings. (AC)

miles of their territory incinerated. This included Kobe's army arsenal and Osaka's industrial district. In neither city did casualties top 5,000 dead. Nagoya proved more stubborn. Two raids only burned out a combined total of 5 square miles.

The fire raids paused because the Twentieth Air Force exhausted its supply of incendiaries. It returned to precision strikes against the aircraft industry until those stocks were replenished. Even then, targets other than Tokyo were chosen for attack.

Tokyo used the respite to clean up. The scale of the damage was so large, cleaning up was all that could be managed. Bodies were discovered and removed for weeks after the raid. So little remained in the worst-hit wards that rebuilding was impossible. Clearing debris from roads represented the best that could be done. Demolition became the priority. In the two weeks following the raid, wide fire lanes were carved through the undamaged wards of Tokyo to serve as firebreaks and open-air fire shelters. The inhabitants of buildings marked for demolition were ordered to evacuate, the buildings knocked down, and the debris carted away.

Evacuation became another priority. Tokyo began evacuating non-essential residents well before air raids began. Although anyone who wanted to leave could do so, priority was given to infants, schoolchildren, pregnant women, and those over 65 years of age. Schoolchildren often evacuated with their classmates, supervised by their teachers. Only a quarter-million of Tokyo's residents opted to evacuate before the capture of the Marianas put Tokyo within range of US bombers. Half moved to outlying parts of Tokyo's prefecture.

The March fire raid accelerated evacuation. Shelter for 1 million homeless was unavailable. Instead, through April 21, non-essential residents of Tokyo were given free railroad transportation to leave Tokyo. Exceptions were individuals essential to air defense and production. Individuals relocating normally needed a Certificate to Change Districts from the municipal government. So many needed to be evacuated after the March 9–10 raid that this paperwork, beloved by the bureaucracy, was waived. It was a clear indication of the urgency of evacuation.

No provision was made for the reception of evacuees. They were to make their own arrangements, or move in with friends or family in the country. This worked surprisingly well. Of the 2.9 million made homeless in Tokyo, nearly 2 million found shelter with friends or family.

Extensive relief efforts were taken to ease the lot of air-raid victims. Starting on March 30, food and clothing was available to those burned out. Refectories were set up in school buildings (vacant due to the evacuation of schoolchildren and available for use) for those unable to prepare their own meals. Food stocks were relocated out of urban areas, dispersed to locations less likely to be burned out in subsequent raids. Relief payments were given to those distressed by the raid. Despite major efforts, the scale of destruction rendered these efforts inadequate.

Replacements were found for the fire engines destroyed and the firefighters killed during the raid. The fire engines were acquired from nearby towns, often by requisitioning. Trainees or volunteers from outside fire departments made up the lost firefighters. These men were less skilled than the men they replaced. Five of Tokyo's 15 main fire stations were destroyed on March 10. They could not be replaced. Tokyo's fire department, inadequate to meet the stresses of March 10, was now even less prepared to deal with another fire raid.

Attempts were made to replace the air defense equipment (including antiaircraft artillery) burned out and personnel killed during the raid. Little was available by way of spare equipment, especially searchlights and gun-laying radar. Most were reassigned from other cities, whose defenses were weakened by their transfer. Trained personnel were scarce and replacements inexperienced.

Using Mount Fuji as the start of a bombing run for a target anywhere in the Tokyo metropolitan area had an important benefit. It meant the bombers were already heading towards the Pacific after dropping their bombs, making it easier for aircrew of damaged aircraft to reach safety. (NMAF)

On April 7, 1945, the Twentieth Air Force mounted a successful attack on the Musashino aircraft engine plant, aided by two firsts: a fighter escort and active ECM. This picture shows the bombs landing in the warehouse and machine shop area, in the east side of the complex. (LOC)

Even before March's fire raid, Tokyo's fighter defenses had been hollowed out. The air battles over Tokyo, especially those during the February 16–17 carrier raid, took their toll on fighter aircraft and aircrew, especially experienced pilots. The Japanese partiality for ramming B-29s removed its most aggressive fighter pilots from the battle. Few survived the first experience; almost none the second. Replacements were thrown into battle with curtailed flight training, lacking the skills needed to survive, much less fight. In all, its defenses had been significantly weakened between November 27, 1944 and April 1, 1945.

Tokyo's respite ended on April 2, as the Twentieth Air Force returned in force. The previous day, the United States, with Allied assistance, invaded Okinawa, a Ryukyu island 500 miles southwest of Kyushu. Okinawa was a Japanese prefecture rather than a colony. It was a part of the Japanese homeland as Hawaii is part of the United States today. Fierce Japanese resistance was expected. Arnold and LeMay were being pressured to use the B-29 to provide tactical support for the operation.

LeMay opposed using his B-29s that way. For him, the best way to "support" the invasion was to redouble strategic bombardment of Japan. He still lacked the incendiaries necessary to resume area bombing. Instead, he chose to target aircraft and aircraft engine factories in Tokyo and Nagoya. He hoped these attacks would draw Japanese aircraft away from Okinawa to defend the factories. If successful, they would cut the numbers of replacement aircraft.

LeMay dispatched a one-wing force of B-29s to hit Musashi. It was a low-altitude nighttime strike, with aircraft departing the Marianas on April 1 and arriving over Musashi between 0300 and 0445hrs. Targeting was done by radar bombsight. It did no worse than previous B-29 daytime raids on Musashi – and no better. One hundred and fifteen B-29s bombed the plant. Dropping 500lb bombs at 5,800 to 8,000ft, they damaged four percent of the buildings, mostly machine shops. Six other B-29s failed to find it and hit urban areas in Tokyo. Of 121 B-29s sent, six failed to return, due to flak damage or mechanical failure.

The Twentieth Air Force conducted a second night raid the following evening. This time, the target was the Tachikawa Aircraft Company's factory. Then Japan's third largest airframe factory, it was located in its namesake town of Tachikawa. Today a Tokyo suburb, in 1945 it was an independent city 20 miles west of downtown Tokyo and 10 miles west of Tokyo's city limits. It produced the Nakajima *Hayabusa* under license, the Tachikawa Ki-54 twin-engine advanced trainer, and was beginning to manufacture the Tachikawa Ki-74, a long-range reconnaissance bomber. It was an important target.

Again, 115 B-29s were dispatched. Only 61 found the primary target. They attacked at altitudes between 6,000 and 8,000ft again, using 500lb general purpose bombs. The Tachikawa plant must have offered a better radar target than Musashi. Despite the relatively small number of B-29s attacking, they did remarkable damage, destroying 243,500sq ft of floor area (including one-fifth of the Ki-74 final assembly building), crippling the sheet metal shop and machine shop, and damaging parts warehouses. The raid delayed Ki-74 production, preventing it from becoming operational by war's end. The remaining bombers hit urban areas in Kawasaki.

Determined to finish off Musashi, LeMay switched back to daylight missions there, launching a mission on April 7. This proved a pivotal day. For the first time, LeMay was launching two major daytime strikes against heavily defended targets. He sent the 313th and 314th Bombardment Wings, 180 aircraft, to attack aircraft factories in Nagoya. The 73rd Wing was sent to hit Musashi, at Tokyo, their tenth mission there. They sent 107 B-29s that day.

Two other major firsts occurred that day. LeMay permitted the B-29's full range of ECM to be used against the Japanese, and the Tokyo force was being accompanied by a fighter escort. The Seventh Air Force sent 108 P-51s from Iwo Jima to escort the Superfortresses.

Seventh Air Force picked its best pilots, men with at least 600 frontline flying hours, to accompany this first mission. They rendezvoused with the B-29s 100 miles east of the Honshu coast, following a B-29 serving as a navigation aircraft. By then, 103 B-29s and 96 P-51s were left. Four B-29s and 12 P-51s had been forced to turn back. The P-51s began providing a close escort of the B-29s, similar to tactics used in Europe.

The 10th Air Division and 71st Air Flotilla scrambled all available aircraft when they received warning of an incoming raid. It was their first real chance to engage B-29s during daylight in over a month. This included scrambling twin-engine night fighters for their firepower. They had also launched Ki-46 reconnaissance bombers to drop air-to-air bombs on the bomber formation. The discovery of the P-51s around the bombers was an unpleasant surprise.

The Mustangs soon engaged the attacking Japanese. A wild melee between Japanese fighters, Japanese bombers, US fighters, and US bombers erupted. Because the Mustangs were stationed close to the bombers, a few Japanese fighters were able to reach the bombers using head-on attacks. Three bombers were shot down by Japanese fighters, including one

B-29s from the 500th Bomb Group of the 73rd Bombardment Wing drop 2,000lb M-66 bombs on the Musashi aircraft engine factory during the April 13, 1945 mission. It was the first use of M-66s in Tokyo, and the bombs easily penetrated the concrete main building. This attack finally scratched Musashino from the target list. (NMAF)

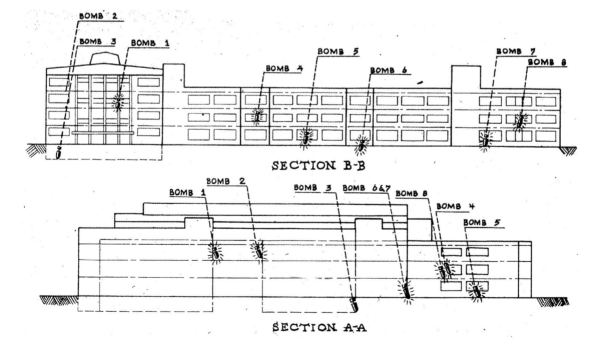

brought down by ramming. The Mustangs were able to drive away most of the Japanese fighters before they could set up attacks.

They made life miserable for the slow night fighters and prevented the Ki-46s from bombing the US formation. When the P-51s landed, they claimed 21 Japanese aircraft destroyed, five probably destroyed, and seven damaged. The claims were almost certainly exaggerated, especially if the 16 kills claimed by B-29 gunners were added in. However, only two Mustangs went down. Even adding in the three bombers lost, the actual exchange rate favored the US.

There were several other differences. The B-29s carried 2,000lb M-66 general purpose bombs for the first time instead of the 500lb M-64 bombs they used on all previous raids. They also bombed from a much lower altitude: 11,500 to 15,650ft. Despite that, only two bombers were lost to flak. Those low losses were due to an often-overlooked, yet important first during that mission: ECM.

ECM is taken for granted today. In 1945, radar, radio direction finding, and similar electronic detection systems were on technology's cutting edge. ECM was even newer; on technology's bleeding edge. The US had developed electronics to jam Japanese gun-laying radar, and installed two different types of jamming transmitters on B-29s: the APT-1 "Dinah" and APQ-2 "Rugs." To prevent development of countermeasures, they had not been used previously. LeMay wanted to wait until there were enough to totally jam the radar and ensure surprise and complete effectiveness in combat.

The B-29s preceded the bomb run by dropping "rope" (long metal strips) from lead bombers in each formation. Dinahs aboard the B-29s barrage-jammed radars, directing flak over the target. Rugs were set to spot jam any radars missed by barrage jamming. Antiaircraft gunners had to lay guns visually, properly setting the altitude of the aircraft. Out of practice, they missed their targets during the critical minutes the bombers were in range.

The results were devastating. The 2,000lb M-66 bombs tore reinforced concrete buildings and fabrication machinery apart. Ten percent of the buildings in the plant were destroyed. Nakajima management decided to abandon the factory, and disperse the undamaged equipment to small, hidden factories elsewhere.

Intelligence officers of the Twentieth Air Force knew Musashi was down, but were not yet convinced it was out. Musashi was revisited by a follow-up raid on April 12. A virtual rerun of the previous raid, 94 B-29s escorted by 90 P-51s struck the factory. M-66 bombs were again used, dropped from 1,000ft higher. The results were better than the previous raid, and Musashi was finally removed from the target list.

Returning to incendiary raids: April 13–16, 1945

Although precision strikes on aircraft factories were finally proving effective, they lacked the impact on curtailing Japanese military production of the first week of fire raids in March. The fire raids ceased because the Twentieth Air Force ran out of incendiaries.

Shortly after assuming command of the Twentieth Air Force, LeMay calculated his needs assuming 735 sorties per wing with 3,200lb of incendiaries per sortie. Instead, they flew 948 sorties with 3,900 tons of incendiaries used, roughly 6,800lb per sortie. This was twice what was planned. The Twentieth Air Force was forced to substitute clusters of 4lb magnesium thermite incendiaries on one mission because they were low on M-47s and M-69s. Magnesium thermite incendiaries were effective against dock areas and heavy industry concentrations, but the M-47 and M-69 were more effective against the wood and bamboo structures that housed home factories than magnesium thermite.

The fire raids, both the demonstration raids conducted by Hansell and LeMay in January and February, and the raids in March, clearly showed fire raids needed saturation for success. Exceed the saturation point and fire prevention services became overwhelmed. They were

forced to allow fires to grow until they burned themselves out. Fail to reach it and the city's fire prevention services contained the fire to the drop area (as they had in the February 25 raid on Tokyo) or even snuffed it out before it spread (which occurred in the fire raid Hansell had sent to Nagoya).

LeMay wanted every fire raid against a major city to be a maximum raid, with all three wings attacking. Three hundred-plus bombers carrying 12,000lb of incendiaries meant a minimum of 1,800 tons of M-47 and M-69 bombs were required per raid. LeMay planned at least a dozen more maximum effort strikes at Japan's six largest cities. That required a lot of munitions. All of it had to be shipped from the US Pacific coast and across the Pacific Ocean to reach the Marianas.

LeMay needed to switch the percentage of incendiary and explosive bombs being shipped. The Twentieth Air Force was expending munitions at higher rates than anticipated. That meant the total bombs tonnage shipped had to increase. That took time. It took nearly three weeks for a ship to steam from the US to the Marianas. For the first month, LeMay had to rely on what was already in the logistics pipeline, in ships already heading to Saipan. Not until mid-April did the Twentieth Air Force accumulate enough incendiaries for LeMay to consider resuming area raids.

On the evening of April 13, the area-bombing campaign resumed. Aircraft from three wings, the 73rd, 113th, and 314th, departed Saipan, Tinian, and Guam. The destination was Tokyo. This time, the target area was Tokyo's arsenal district, north of the Imperial Palace complex and west of the area bombed on March 10. It was an important industrial district.

Logistics dominated the B-29 campaign. Superfortresses dropped large numbers of bombs, all of which had to come from America's west coast. Initially, too many M-64 500lb bombs, like the ones shown, and too few incendiaries were shipped. Changing the ratio of incendiaries to general purpose bombs and increasing the number of munitions sent took six weeks. (NMAF)

The ECM position in a B-29 was stuffed to one side of the forward upper turret. First used in April 1945, ECM blinded Japan's gun-laying radar, permitting the successful destruction of the Musashino engine factor, and allowed two fire raids on Tokyo to occur with almost no loss. (NMAF)

It contained the headquarters of the First and Second Tokyo Arsenals, two of six Imperial Army Arsenals. Between them, they produced 40 percent of the production of the Imperial Army Arsenal system in 1944 and one-third of it in 1945. Army-controlled plants in the target zone produced a large fraction of the Imperial Army's small arms ammunition, radios and radar systems, fuses for antiaircraft shells, and much of the Army's smokeless, yellow and brown powder.

These were surrounded by a multitude of home factories, many producing the parts and subassemblies feeding the arsenal factories. It was made up of Tokyo's Kanda, Shitaya, Arakawa, and Hongo wards. While not as built up as the Asakusa, it was still densely populated. The first three wards had a population density of 80,000 to 135,000 residents per square mile. Hongo's density was 50,000 to 80,000 residents per square mile.

The raid was a virtual repeat of the March fire raid. The pathfinders arrived shortly after midnight, and blazed a flaming mark in the target area. It served as an aiming point for the bombers that followed over the next three hours. Soon, there were too many fires for Tokyo's fire department to contain. The flames soon started spreading uncontrollably.

There were no rivers to serve as firebreaks. Only the main railyard proved wide and open enough to stop the spreading flames. That did not matter, however. Bombers dropped incendiaries on both sides of the firebreak. By then, the fire department was fully committed, and had no engines to spare fighting these new fires.

Fires also scattered over a wider area than during the previous raid. Some crews dropped their loads all over the northern half of Tokyo, ignoring the areas already burning. This was probably done by the later crews. They may have decided that the fires were so widespread no one was available to stop the fires they started. Some dropped loads well east of the aiming point, possibly to turn homeward sooner. Fortunately for Tokyo, the high winds of March 10 were absent. This raid did not trigger another firestorm.

Of 330 B-29s sent, 327 reached Tokyo. It was the largest raid yet to strike Tokyo. They dropped 4,500,000lb of incendiaries on Tokyo that night. By the time the fires died out, another 11.4 square miles of Tokyo were smoldering ruins. Production of critical munitions ground to a halt. Stored small arms, machine guns, and artillery were destroyed. Ordinance production dropped one-quarter. Casualties mercifully were lighter: 2,500 dead and 4,700 wounded, a precipitous drop from the 124,000 killed and wounded in March. Another 170,500 buildings were destroyed and nearly 650,000 Tokyo residents rendered homeless. It was another calamitous blow to Tokyo.

For the Twentieth Air Force, this was one of the safest fire missions flown. Only seven B-29s failed to return. Electronic countermeasures blinded Japanese radar, rendering antiaircraft artillery and night fighters impotent. The Japanese still had found no way to counter the jamming.

The Twentieth Air Force set out to revisit Tokyo only one day after this second Tokyo fire raid. This time, the target was southern Tokyo and Kawasaki, immediately south of Tokyo. Sandwiched between Tokyo and Yokohama, Kawasaki was an industrial town. In 1940, it had a population of over 300,000. It held the most important industrial concentration in the Tokyo urban area.

Kawasaki played the same role to Tokyo that Warren, Michigan then filled for Detroit. It was where the heavy industry was concentrated. Kawasaki was filled with factories, foundries, and refineries. These were traditional targets for precision bombing. On April 14–15, the Twentieth Air Force was going to attempt to destroy them by burning them out.

This time, 303 B-29s were sent. The pathfinders arrived at their target shortly after midnight on April 15. One wing with 109 B-29s hit southern Tokyo. The other two wings, 194 strong, hit Kawasaki. This time, the pathfinders marked multiple aiming points in the two cities. They dropped a total of 1,930 tons of incendiaries on both cities.

The Tokyo portion of the raid fell most heavily in the wards beside Tokyo Bay, filled with docks and warehouses, and on the wards along Tokyo's southern limits. This region had some of the lowest population densities in Tokyo, from 30,000 to 50,000 people per square mile or less. It burned perhaps a little better than the more densely packed arsenal area. This time, 6 square miles of Tokyo burned down. Warehouses, storage facilities, and office buildings were the primary casualties, rather than manufacturing facilities. The stored goods incinerated within would be badly missed because within a month they would become irreplaceable. Some manufacturing plants were destroyed. The Fuji Aircraft Company, which built training aircraft, had a factory in Tokyo's Kamata Ward, across the Tama River from Kawasaki. It was burned out during the raid.

Kawasaki lost only 3.6 square miles to incendiaries, but the fires burned out the industrial heart of the city. Several aircraft manufacturing companies had headquarters buildings in Kawasaki. Several, including Mitaka Aircraft Industries, were burned out. Mitaka, which built carburetors, oil pumps, and fuel pumps, had the factories producing these destroyed as well. Hitachi Aircraft Company, which built aircraft engines, had a foundry in Kawasaki. It produced cylinder castings for Tachikawa and for its own engine factories

The April 14–15 fire raid was the third that hit the Tokyo urban area. Targeted were both Kawasaki on Tokyo's southern boundary and Tokyo wards next to Kawasaki by Tokyo Bay. Many warehouses by the docks in this part of Tokyo's harbor were burned out during the raid. (AC)

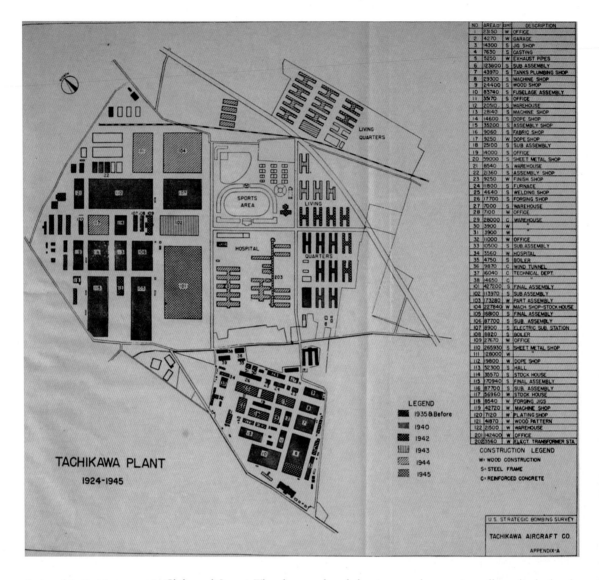

A plan of the Tachikawa Aircraft Factory. It was the third-largest airframe plant in Japan. It produced the Ki-54 advanced trainer, the Ki-43 *Hayabusa* (under license), and the Ki-72 reconnaissance bomber. It was hit by the US Navy in February, and closed after the B-29 raid in April. (AC)

in Chiba and Omori. The plant produced aluminum and magnesium alloy cylinder heads, reduction gear housings, crankcases, and casings for distributors, oil and fuel pumps, and carburetors. It was burned out during this raid. The Tama River, dividing Tokyo from Kawasaki, served as a firebreak, but at several points incendiaries fell on both sides of it, jumping the firebreak.

The raid on Kawasaki spilled over to Yokohama, bordering Kawasaki's southern city limits. Yokohama had 1.6 square miles burned out before bringing the fires within its limits under control. Some 50,000 buildings in Tokyo and Yokohama burned down. Kawasaki lost 31,600 buildings.

Measured by destruction per aircraft, the bombers which hit Tokyo that night were 50 percent more effective than two nights earlier. This despite the area hit being less densely built up than in the previous two fire raids. Possibly this was because the part of Tokyo bombed that night had not previously been bombed, and there was no previous damage to serve as firebreaks. It was also possible that Tokyo's fire department was less efficient than it had been two nights earlier. The previous raid destroyed equipment, and exhausted fire department personnel had not had time to recover.

Fires failed to spread as widely in Kawasaki due to the nature of the targets. Foundries, large industrial plants, and refineries of concrete and metal construction burned well, but fires set there failed to spread. Neighboring structures, also concrete and metal, were less likely to be set ablaze by an adjacent building than densely packed wooden structures.

Those were the last fire raids for nearly a month. Two factors accounted for this. Incendiary stocks were low. The two raids consumed over 4,000 tons of incendiaries. That was roughly equivalent to what had been delivered since the last round of fire raids. Increased deliveries of incendiaries were only just beginning to arrive at the Marianas.

Another reason was LeMay had been forced to pull off his B-29s to attack tactical targets. The April 1 invasion of Okinawa required the US Navy to maintain a large fleet off the Ryukyus to support the landings. Japan was launching frequent and massive kamikaze attacks on these ships from airfields in Kyushu. The US Navy had been taking unprecedented casualties. Twentieth Air Force bombers were the only means of hitting these airfields. The Navy wanted them bombed, to prevent their use as bases for kamikaze attacks.

Arnold and LeMay initially resisted using B-29s to attack airfields. They felt the B-29s were incapable of closing the airfields by bombing. Two weeks of incessant US Navy losses forced them to yield to US Navy demands. Starting April 17, the Twentieth Air Force began attacking Kyushu airfields. They spent the next three weeks futilely trying to suppress the kamikazes by bombing their bases. Japan's cities, including Tokyo, gained a respite.

There was only one break in this campaign. LeMay was allowed to attack strategic targets when the Kyushu airfields were clouded over. The Kyushu April skies remained as relentlessly clear as the winter Tokyo skies had been rainy. The first opportunity to interrupt the airfield interlude came on April 24, over a week after the last visit to Tokyo.

The target was Tachikawa, a follow-up to the April 3 attack. This time, 101 B-29s were sent. It was another medium-altitude daylight strike. It was an advertisement for precision bombing. Damage was extensive. The main subassembly building for producing the *Hayabusa* was destroyed, as was the parts assembly building. The wing assembly jigs in the parts assembly building were damaged. The undamaged parts of the machine shop hit in the April 3 raid were destroyed. Floor area damaged totaled 570,000sq ft, over twice the damage of the April 3 raid. The Imperial Army ordered the factory closed, dispersing the surviving equipment.

Water and fire: May 5 to 29, 1945

Tachikawa was the last bombing raid on Tokyo for nearly a month, but was not the last visit by B-29s to Tokyo during that period. A mission to Tokyo flown the night of May 4–5 had dramatic consequences for the Tokyo urban area, although no bombs fell anywhere near it.

Unlike Hansell, LeMay was enthusiastic about using B-29s to lay mines in Japanese waterways. Hansell viewed minelaying as a distraction from strategic bombing. LeMay saw it as an adjunct to it, a different form of strategic application of air power. In March, he started the first phase of Operation *Starvation*, a campaign to isolate Japan from outside resources by closing its seaports and waterways with air-dropped mines. LeMay devoted the 313th Bombardment Wing to mine-dropping, using them exclusively for those missions. Phase I, which started on March 27, concentrated on closing down the Shimonoseki Strait, separating Kyushu and Honshu to channelize the Imperial Navy using Inland Sea ports into using the Bungo Suido. Since the Shimonoseki Strait was Japan's busiest maritime passageway, it had the added effect of choking off supplies coming from Korea or the China Seas. It proved an outstanding success.

Phase II, which started on May 3, was the Industrial Center Blockade. Its goal was to destroy seaborne communications to Japan's great cities: Tokyo, Nagoya, Kobe, Osaka, and Yokohama. In part, this was to be done by mining the approaches to these seaports. To add

An armorer oversees the loading of a sea mine into a 313th Wing B-29 during Operation *Starvation*. This is a 2,000lb Mark 25. Only aircraft from the 313th Bombardment Wing, trained in their deployment, were used to drop these mines. They closed Japanese ports, including Yokohama and Tokyo, to ocean-going ships. (NMAF)

to their effectiveness, these new mines were fused with a new pressure fuse. It was believed to be "unsweepable," impossible to remove through conventional minesweeping.

Most of the Phase II mines were laid in the Inland Sea, to prevent access to the ports ringing its shores. The second mission of Phase II was aimed at closing Japan's two biggest ports outside the Inland Sea, Tokyo and Yokohama. On the evening of May 5, while the rest of the Twentieth Air Force was busy elsewhere in Japan, 90 aircraft of the 313th Wing departed Tinian for Tokyo.

They carried, a mixture of 2,000lb Mark 25 mines and 1,000lb Marks 26 and 36 mines; 810 in all. Eighty-six aircraft reached Tokyo Bay and the approaches to it. (Four others found targets of opportunity elsewhere off the Home Islands.) They dropped their mines in a carefully coordinated pattern, using radar navigation to assure precise placement. Before dawn broke, relieved of their loads, they were heading back to Tinian.

The residents of the Tokyo urban complex must have felt relief that night. The air-raid alerts must have sounded when Japanese early warning radar detected incoming Superfortresses. But no bombs fell on Tokyo that night. The air-raid warning sirens, heralding another incendiary raid, remained silent.

The realization of what had been done dawned slowly, when ships entering or departing Tokyo Bay began striking mines. Minesweeping attempts proved ineffective. Shipping dropped by 50 percent in May, and another 50 percent in June. Raw materials and finished goods had to depend on rail thereafter. Industries dropped production levels due to shortages of raw materials.

Nimitz released the Twentieth Air Force from airfield suppression on May 11. LeMay immediately turned his attention to strategic bombardment, including resuming the incendiary campaign. He also had one more B-29 wing available. The 58th Bombardment Wing, transferred from the China–Burma–India Theater, became fully operational on May 5.

The airfield break permitted the Twentieth to stockpile incendiaries. Since March, an increased percentage of the munitions shipped to the Marianas were incendiaries and the overall tonnage of munitions had increased. There would be no further pauses in incendiary raids due to shortages. With four wings, they would be larger, 400 to 550 aircraft. Nagoya and Hamamatsu (an industrial city southwest of Tokyo) felt the first fury of the fire raids. On May 23, it was Tokyo's turn again.

Just before sunset, May 23, 562 B-29s from four different B-29 wings lifted off runways in Saipan, Tinian, and Guam. All headed to Tokyo, the largest number of B-29s sent to attack a single target to date. It would turn out to be the largest concentration of B-29s to attack one city in the whole war. The target area for this raid was a district south of the Imperial Palace, immediately north of the sector bombed on April 15. It too contained a mixture of industrial plants and residential communities, and included docks and warehouses on Tokyo Bay's western shore. It also had a population density that ranged between 30,000 and 50,000 residents per square mile.

Visibility was poor. Tokyo had 9/10th cloud cover that night due to low clouds. Most aircraft, including the 44 pathfinders, used radar bombing. As before, they carried M-47 incendiaries, with subsequent waves armed with M-69s. The bombers came in from the south at altitudes between 7,800 and 15,000ft. The pathfinders marked the targets while following waves dropped their loads outside the areas currently ablaze. By May 23, it was a well-practiced drill. Even the newly arrived 58th Wing had flown three incendiary missions by May 23.

The results were solid, but not spectacular. Five hundred and twenty Superfortresses made it to Tokyo. (Five others hit targets of opportunity outside the Tokyo area.) They scattered 3,646 tons of incendiaries over the target area. The scale of the attack went beyond the capabilities of Tokyo's fire department to handle. What had been inadequate to deal with 320 fire-bombing B-29s was even less adequate when half-again that number attacked. All the firefighters could do was get out of the path of the worst of the fire and attempt to contain it from spreading too far. The raid burned out another 5.3 square miles of Tokyo, including areas missed during the April 16 raid.

The high winds of March were absent and a firestorm did not occur. By May, Tokyo residents had become as practiced in evacuating from raids as the B-29 crews were in executing them. Perhaps 1,500 died on the ground that night. The bombers paid the highest price they had to date, however. A total of 17 B-29s were lost that night; 13 were shot down, and four were operational losses. Sixty-nine B-29s were damaged by antiaircraft fire.

Flak was fierce over Tokyo. Japanese air defense forces found means of coping with the effects of radar jamming. There were also more targets overhead to shoot at: 502 on this raid versus the 279 which attacked on March 19. Since 14 were lost to flak on March 10, it could even be argued Tokyo's antiaircraft batteries were less effective than two months earlier. The raid yielded a 3.3 percent loss rate, acceptable even if it was higher than that of the April fire raids.

The Twentieth Air Force returned two nights later. This time, the target area was the city immediately south and west of the Imperial Palace. In addition to the factories and residential quarters bombed in earlier raids, it included Tokyo's financial, commercial, and governmental districts. It was the heart of the Empire's administrative state and its commercial headquarters. It included the largest and most modern buildings in Tokyo.

The attack was a virtual repeat of the previous raid, with the bombers using the same altitudes from which to bomb. Approach and departure routes were modified to avoid the worst of the flak. This time, 502 aircraft left the Marianas and 464 reached Tokyo.

A Japanese cameraman captures B-29s flying over the Tokyo urban area during a raid in May 1945. Black puffs of flak can be seen below the bombers. Although labeled as a raid occurring on May 25, that was a night attack. This probably shows the daylight fire raid on Yokohama of May 29. (Wikimedia)

The final Tokyo-area fire raid

On May 29, 1945 the Twentieth Air Force launched its sixth and final fire raid against the Tokyo urban area. The target was Yokohama, at the southern end of the metropolitan area, and Japan's sixth largest city. A rare daytime fire raid, it completed the Tokyo area's destruction.

Key:

──────── Japanese aircraft

──────── US aircraft

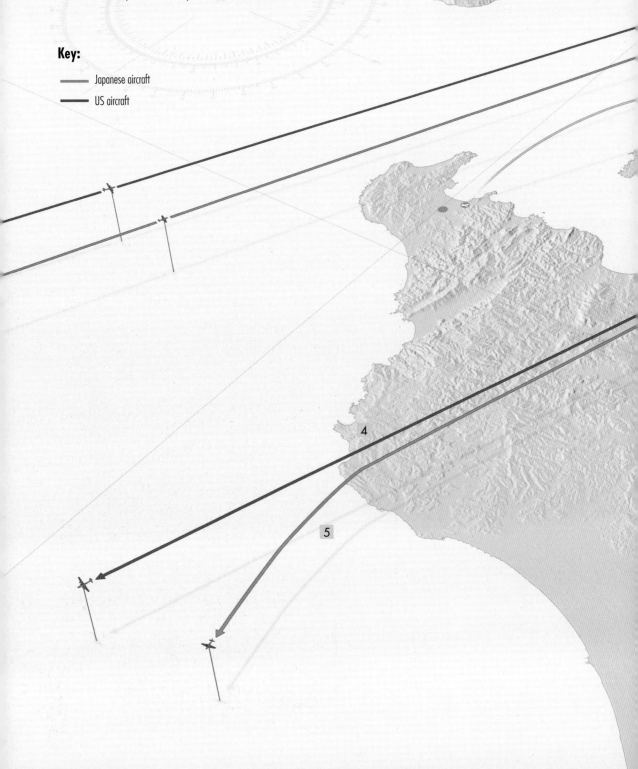

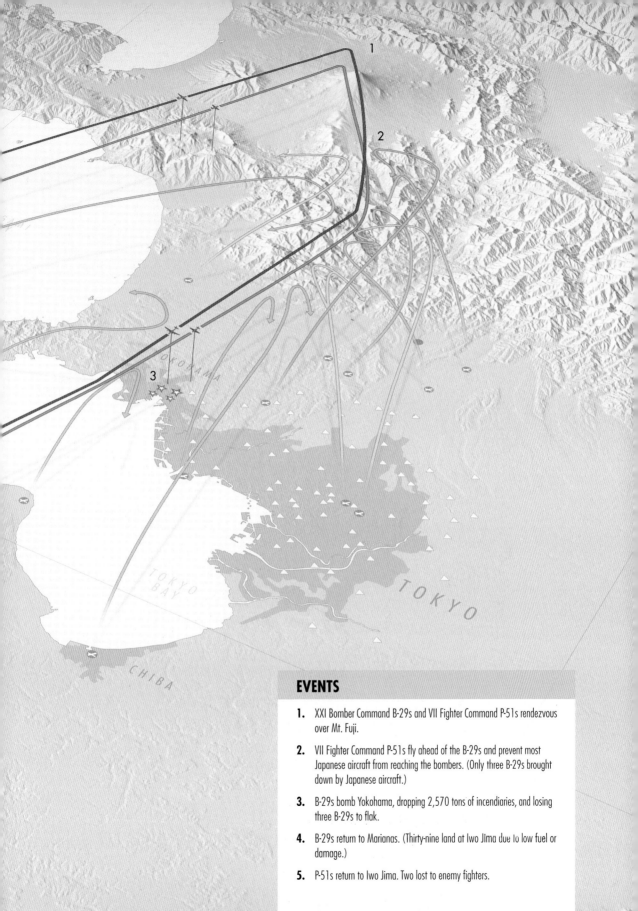

EVENTS

1. XXI Bomber Command B-29s and VII Fighter Command P-51s rendezvous over Mt. Fuji.

2. VII Fighter Command P-51s fly ahead of the B-29s and prevent most Japanese aircraft from reaching the bombers. (Only three B-29s brought down by Japanese aircraft.)

3. B-29s bomb Yokohama, dropping 2,570 tons of incendiaries, and losing three B-29s to flak.

4. B-29s return to Marianas. (Thirty-nine land at Iwo Jima due to low fuel or damage.)

5. P-51s return to Iwo Jima. Two lost to enemy fighters.

The commercial district of Tokyo was left in shambles by a fire raid on May 24–25. Although this image was taken during the occupation of Japan, it captures the result of the May 24–25 fire raid that burned out this part of Tokyo along with the adjacent government district. (LOC)

Six others hit targets of opportunity. Pathfinders blazed out aim points used by the aircraft that followed. This night, there was only 3/10th cloud cover and the early waves bombed visually. Late waves were forced to use radar bombing as smoke obscured the target area.

The bombers dropped 3,262 tons of incendiaries that night. It burned out the last remaining part of Tokyo of strategic interest. In all, 16.8 square miles were destroyed before the fires died out. This was the largest area wiped out on any Tokyo raid. The two May raids destroyed a combined total of 155,000 buildings. In all, 3,200 were killed and 13,700 injured, with 550,000 being rendered homeless, half the number from the March raid, despite more square miles being burned out in May. This reflected the lower percentage of residences in the May target area. It hit many more low-occupancy offices and warehouses.

It was also the most fiercely fought incendiary raid of the war. Desperate to protect their city, the 10th Air Division sent up single-engine day fighters as well as night fighters to intercept the bombers. Antiaircraft fire was the heaviest experienced during any Tokyo raid. Losses totaled 26 B-29s shot down (mostly by flak) and 100 damaged. B-29 gunners claimed 19 Japanese fighters shot down. Yet the losses were worth it. The city of Tokyo was removed from the target list.

The Twentieth Air Force however was not yet done with the Tokyo urban area. Although Tokyo and Kawasaki were torched, Yokohama had only experienced the spillover from the April 16 raid on Kawasaki. Most of it remained intact. Although Operation *Starvation* had erased its utility as a seaport, it remained a major industrial and manufacturing center. It was also Japan's sixth largest city. Except for Kyoto, spared for cultural reasons, Yokohama was the only major city not yet hit by the fury of a US Army Air Force fire raid.

On May 29, LeMay sent 517 B-29s to flatten Yokohama. It was much different than previous incendiary raids. Concerned about losses over Tokyo in May, LeMay changed tactics. This raid was a daylight mission. The bombers would attack from high altitude to mitigate the effectiveness of Japanese antiaircraft fire. They would also be escorted. One hundred and one P-51s from the Seventh Air Force's VII Fighter Command were dispatched from Iwo Jima to protect the bombers from Japanese fighters.

The weather was good, and the Mustangs rendezvoused with the B-29s over Mount Fuji, southwest of Tokyo. By then, the Superfortress numbers were down to 454, thinned out as bombers with mechanical problems returned to the Marianas or made emergency landings at Iwo Jima. The P-51s placed themselves ahead and 2,000ft above the bombers. Then the formation turned east to Yokohama. Both the 10th Air Division and the 302nd Air Group turned out in force to stop the B-29s, 150 strong.

A massive aerial brawl broke out at 22,000ft. The Mustangs intercepted Japanese fighters short of the bombers. They claimed 26 Japanese fighters shot down, six damaged, and 23 probably shot down. While the claims were probably excessive, they were not overly exaggerated. Few Japanese fighters got through the P-51 screen to attack the bombers. Between flak and fighters, only seven B-29s were shot down, one of which was brought down by ramming. It was the last B-29 lost to ramming. Three Mustangs were lost.

The bombers flew over Yokohama boosted by the jet stream. Winds scattered the bombs as they fell to earth. What worked to foil high-altitude precision bombing accuracy aided an area raid. The scattering ensured the type of widely and evenly distributed coverage desired in an incendiary raid. The 2,570 tons of incendiaries dropped burned out 6.9 square miles of Yokohama. The third of the city destroyed included Yokohama's main business district and the waterfront. Including the damage from the May raid, 44 percent of Yokohama was in ruins. Yokohama was struck from the target list.

B-29s from the 499th Bomb Group of the 73rd Bombardment Wing release incendiary bombs on Yokohama in May 1945. It was a rare daytime fire raid, with the B-29s escorted by fighters. Note the jet stream winds scattering the incendiary clusters as they fell. (NMAF)

To the end: June–August, 1945

For all practical purposes, the campaign against Tokyo ended with the Yokohama raid of May 29. The United States won. The six fire raids leveled 68.8 square miles of the Tokyo urban area, nearly 50 percent of the built-up area. The major aircraft factories around Tokyo were ruined. The Tokyo urban area had been destroyed as a center of production and crippled as an administrative center. The war was not over. Battles over and around Tokyo continued.

The Twentieth Air Force launched six more raids against the Tokyo area before the war ended. All were against industrial targets, aircraft factories, and oil refineries. None involved more than a wing, during a period when the Twentieth Air Force had five B-29 wings available. None contributed significantly to Allied victory. They were either technology tests or intended to make absolutely sure a factory was not being repaired.

The first was on June 10, when 29 B-29s were sent against the Imperial Army's Air Arsenal at Tachikawa, adjacent to the aircraft factory there. It was previously damaged by spillover from the air raids on the factory. Additionally, a major function was to receive aircraft from the Tachikawa aircraft factory. After the factory was disrupted by bombing, the Air Arsenal had little remaining purpose. By June, the Twentieth Air Force had no better target, so they dropped 169 tons of general purpose 500lb bombs on it.

The 315th Bombardment Wing became operational in early June. Its B-29s were equipped with the AN/APQ-7 Eagle radar, more accurate than the AN/APQ-13 radar installed on the other B-29s. It could not resolve targets the size of an aircraft factory, but was capable of permitting precision bombing of large installations such as oil refineries or shipyards.

The AN/APQ-7 Eagle radar permitted nighttime precision bombing of large targets like oil refineries. B-29s of the 315th Bombardment Wing used it to smash oil refineries in the Tokyo area during three missions in July and August 1945. These refineries could store 1.2 million barrels of oil. Eliminating stored oil was as important as eliminating oil production. (LOC)

Accuracy required a long, straight run-up to the target, making radar-guided daytime attacks inadvisable. The 315th, like the 313th, became a specialist wing. It conducted nighttime radar-directed precision bombing. By June 1945, Japan had virtually abandoned shipbuilding, so its missions were almost exclusively against oil refineries.

Three raids were conducted in the Tokyo area, all against targets in Kawasaki. These refineries accounted for one-quarter of Japan's domestic production. The first occurred on the night of July 11–12. The target was the Kawasaki Petroleum Center, located on an artificial island on the Kawasaki waterfront. It could refine 2 million barrels of petroleum annually and its tanks could store 1.2 million barrels. Sixty aircraft were sent, and 53 bombed, dropping 1,808 500lb general purpose bombs on the easily identified target. The raid destroyed 25 percent of the refinery and storage tanks, rendering it unusable. Flak, although heavy, was ineffective due to cloud cover. One aircraft was lost shortly after take-off and one B-29 was lost during the mission.

The 315th returned to Kawasaki on July 26, hitting the Mitsubishi Oil Company and Hayama Petroleum Center, and on August 2, revisiting all three earlier targets. On July 26, 83 B-29s attacked, dropping 650 tons of 500lb bombs, and destroying one-third of their target. That time, flak shot down one B-29, scoring a direct hit. On August 1, 128 B-29s launched with 120 reaching their targets after midnight on August 2. They dropped 1,100 tons of bombs. No aircraft were lost on that mission, although 26 were hit by antiaircraft fire that night. At the end of these three missions, 41 percent of the Mitsubishi Oil Company, 43 percent of the Hayama Petroleum Center, and nearly 50 percent of the Kawasaki Petroleum Center had been destroyed.

The most unusual attack against Tokyo occurred on July 29 when a lone B-29 dropped one 12,000lb bomb on Musashi. The target was unimportant. It was a practice atomic mission. The B-29 was *Bockscar*, an aircraft of the 509th Composite Group. The bomb was a "pumpkin bomb," identical in shape and weight to the "Fat Man" atomic bomb dropped on Hiroshima, but filled with conventional explosives.

On August 8, the Twentieth Air Force made one last raid on Musashi, ending the Tokyo raids where they began. This was two days after the Hiroshima bomb and the day before Nagasaki. There was little at the Musashino factory, but it served to remind the capital of US air power, an attempt to convince Japan to surrender following the Hiroshima bombing. Sixty B-29s set out; 51 reached Musashino and dropped 289 2,000lb M-66 bombs on the wrecked and abandoned factory. It was a demonstration of how to make rubble bounce.

None were seriously opposed by Japanese air forces, either the Imperial Army's or the Imperial Navy's. By then, Japan had severe shortages of fuel due to the US Navy's blockade of Japan and Operation *Starvation*. In June, Imperial Headquarters began hoarding what aircraft were left to allow a massive aerial counterattack when the inevitable Allied invasion came. Shooting down B-29s, even those over Tokyo would not stop the invasion. The remaining aircraft defending Tokyo were scattered to remote fields, dispersed, and hidden, with only token opposition sent against the raids.

Other US forces also came to Tokyo in the war's final months, most notably the Seventh Air Force and Task Force 38. Both entities launched attacks on the Tokyo area in July and August.

The reluctance of Japanese fighters to engage B-29s over the Home Islands reduced escort duties for P-51s stationed in Iwo Jima. These were part of the Seventh Air Force's VII Fighter Command. They were still needed occasionally, but Seventh Air Force leaders felt the Mustangs were underemployed. Rather than have them sit on the ground idle, they decided to use them for fighter sweeps. Tokyo was the closest part of the Home Islands to Iwo Jima, so it was a natural target.

The distance meant Mustangs could not carry a bombload. Carrying bombs prevented them from carrying drop tanks. The six .50cal machine guns they had made strafing an

The Imperial air forces began refusing to engage US aircraft after June. Instead, Japanese warplanes were dispersed and hidden to repel the expected Allied invasion of the Home Islands. To reduce the number of potential kamikazes that day and to keep their P-51s occupied, the Seventh Air Force instead employed Iwo Jima-based P-51s conducting fighter sweeps against Japanese airfields around Tokyo. (AC)

effective means of destroying ground targets. They were powerful enough to punch through locomotive boilers, hangers, warehouses, and oil storage tanks, all worthwhile targets.

On July 4, 1945, the Seventh Air Force celebrated American Independence Day by sending 159 P-51s from Iwo Jima to airfields in and around Tokyo. The fighters provided fireworks at the Imperial Navy's Yokosuka and Tsukuba airfields and the Imperial Army's satellite Chiba Airfield. They shot up ground facilities and any aircraft spotted at the airfields. The returning pilots claimed nine aircraft destroyed on the ground and 26 damaged. One P-51 was lost.

Over the next two days, two more fighter sweeps were made against Tokyo-area airfields. On July 5, 100 P-51s swept across the Kantō Plain, attacking airfields as far away as 50 miles from Tokyo. They claimed six more Japanese aircraft destroyed on the ground with 11 damaged, and returned without loss. On July 6, 111 P-51s participated. This time, one aerial kill was claimed, with six on the ground claimed destroyed and 25 damaged. One P-51 was downed.

Next was the US Navy's turn. The Fast Carrier Force, renumbered Task Force 38, began a six-week carrier raid along the coast of Japan's Home Islands. Their strikes ranged the Pacific coast of Japan from Hokkaido to Shikoku. They opened the attack with strikes on Tokyo on July 10. Commanding was Halsey, now Fleet Admiral. It was the first time he had attacked Tokyo since the Doolittle Raid three years earlier. Instead of two fleet carriers and 16 bombers, Halsey had nine fleet carriers, six light carriers, and 1,100 aircraft. The attack took the Japanese by surprise.

The carrier aircraft swept over the Kantō Plain, attacking every airfield they could find. It was a wide-ranging attack, striking airfields as far as 50 miles from Tokyo. The bombers were armed primarily with fragmentation bombs to destroy aircraft. The weather was good, and they worked over the airfields most of the day. The US Navy owned the skies. No Japanese aircraft took to the air; most were hidden in camouflaged revetments. All Japanese aircraft were viewed as targets. The Japanese were putting bombs in trainers to use as kamikazes. That day's attack may have damaged or destroyed over 200 aircraft; exact numbers were never determined.

At dark, TF38 pulled east, refueled, and spent the next week attacking Northern Honshu and Hokkaido, bombarding both with warplanes and battleships. On July 17, it was back off to Tokyo, but the planned airstrikes were scrubbed due to foul weather. The weather cleared enough the next day to permit carrier operations. That day's targets were more airfields plus shipping and warships in and around Tokyo Bay.

Yokosuka was a particular target that day. US Navy aircraft worked over the Yokosuka shipyard, and hunted Imperial Navy warships in and around it. They sank the destroyer *Yaezakura*, submarine *I-372*, two escort vessels, a torpedo boat, and five smaller vessels.

The big prize that day was *Nagato*, the Imperial Navy's most modern surviving battleship. Although hidden against the shoreline and heavily camouflaged, US carrier planes found it. The first waves of US Navy aircraft sent against it took out the antiaircraft guns protecting the battleship with coordinated airstrikes. Then F6F fighter bombers plastered it with bombs, damaging it badly enough to require a shipyard for repairs. After this, TF38 hauled out to hit Imperial Navy bases further south on the Home Islands.

The Seventh Air Force returned on July 28 with another fighter sweep. It sent over 140 P-51s to strafe airfields and other military targets around Tokyo. Two more fighter sweeps, with around 100 P-51s, were flown on August 3 and August 6. They added railroad installations and trains to the mix of airfields and military installations, as the US began to shift focus to Japan's transportation network.

The Japanese battleship *Nagato* was the Imperial Navy's most powerful remaining warship in July 1945. By then, it was sheltering in Tokyo Bay, attempting to survive until the invasion, which it would oppose. During US Navy raids on Tokyo Bay on July 7, 1945, US Navy warplanes hunted it down and crippled it. (AC)

AFTERMATH AND ANALYSIS

The last air combat over Tokyo occurred three days after hostilities officially ceased. Four B-32s conducting a photoreconnaissance mission over Tokyo Bay were attacked by Japanese fighters whose pilots impulsively attacked the bombers, despite the war having ended. The bombers' gunners drove off the attacking fighters, but one Dominator was written off after returning to base. (NMAF)

On August 6, the US dropped an atomic bomb on Hiroshima. On August 9, *Bockscar*, which bombed Musashino 11 days earlier, dropped a "Little Boy" atomic bomb on Nagasaki. In between those events, the Soviet Union declared war on Japan. The next day, August 10, Imperial Japan sued for peace.

Japan began haggling over what surrender meant. As a result, Halsey decided to use TF38 to increase pressure on Japan. He scheduled airstrikes on Tokyo for August 11. Foul weather postponed the strikes until August 13, when it launched a series of deckload strikes on Tokyo. The Fast Carrier Force refueled that evening, finishing on the morning of August 14. By 1415hrs, TF38 launched a new set of strikes towards Tokyo, followed by a second wave an hour later.

The first wave were approaching their targets when Halsey got the word to suspend further operations. Follow-on strikes were canceled and the two airborne waves recalled. One group of six Hellcats was over a Japanese airfield when the recall came. They were jumped by 15 Japanese aircraft. A wild melee saw four Hellcats and nine Japanese aircraft go down.

The following day, the war ended. Halsey announced the war's end to the Third Fleet radioing: "Cessation of hostilities. War is over. If any Japanese airplanes appear, shoot them down in a friendly way." It was a necessary precaution. Many Japanese aviators were unwilling to end hostilities, even at their Emperor's direction. Die-hards launched kamikaze attacks that day. They were intercepted and shot down, presumably in a friendly way, before they did damage.

For two weeks, Japan remained unoccupied and armed, awaiting a formal surrender. It led to an interesting coda to the battle for Tokyo. The US, distrustful of Japanese sincerity and seeking reassurance no threat was posed to the Allied fleet scheduled to arrive at Tokyo, flew reconnaissance flights over Tokyo.

The aircraft used were B-32 Dominators, originally ordered as a potential replacement for the B-29 had development of that aircraft failed. Instead, B-32 development stalled, the aircraft not arriving until the last months of the war. Inferior to the B-29 and available only in small numbers, they were converted to photoreconnaissance aircraft.

Four flew over Tokyo on August 17. This proved too much for Imperial Army and Navy fighter pilots near Tokyo. Antiaircraft artillery from Yokosuka greeted the Dominators as they flew over the Yokosuka Naval Base. A swarm of fighters intercepted the Dominators. The two sides exchanged fire. Although damaged by Japanese fire, all four B-32s returned to safe landings at Okinawa. One was so badly damaged it was written off. B-32 gunners claimed one fighter downed. With that anomalous encounter, the battle for Tokyo ended. On September 2, 1945, the Third Fleet entered Tokyo Bay, and Japan signed the instruments of surrender.

Who won? Clearly, the United States. On November 27, 1944, when the Twentieth Air Force launched its first attack on Tokyo, Tokyo was a thriving industrial city with a population of 6.6 million spread over an area of 223 square miles. Of this, 110.6 square miles had urban density. On August 10, 1945, its population was down to 2.3 million. Nearly 100,000 had died in the bombing, and 4.1 million had evacuated. Of its urban area, 56.3 square miles, over half, had been burned out, leaving 2.8 million homeless.

That was just in Tokyo. Yokohama's population had dropped from 1 million to 637,000, with 8.9 square miles of its 22.2 square miles of urban area in ashes. Kawasaki's population went from 380,000 to 216,000 with a loss of 6.7 of its 11.0 square miles of urban area. There were far fewer deaths in those cities, 4,800 in Yokohama and 1,500 in Kawasaki, but over 550,000 people in both cities lost their homes. Combined, the urban complex went from 8 million inhabitants to 3.2 million in ten months. In total, 68.8 square miles had been burned out, and 863,000 buildings, from single-family homes to modern office buildings, had been destroyed. Ninety percent of that damage had occurred on and after March 10, 1945.

The victory was largely due to the Twentieth Air Force. Task Force 38 did serious damage during its raids on February 15–17 and July 10–11, 1945. The Seventh Air Force fighter sweeps also contributed. However, the smallest B-29 fire raid, that of March 10, 1945, did more damage to the Tokyo urban area than all the TF38 carrier strikes and Seventh Air Force fighter sweeps of the war, with the damage of all previous Twentieth Air Force raids on Tokyo combined. (The February 1945 US Navy raids also did more damage to Tokyo than all previous Twentieth Air Force raids on Tokyo.)

The Twentieth Air Force had one of the most dramatic turnarounds in military history. Up until March 8, 1945, Japan was winning the battle for Tokyo. The Twentieth Air Force had done virtually no damage up to that point. The raid of February 25, when three wings

By war's end, Tokyo had been reduced to ruins. Its population was one quarter the size it had been when the war began. Those who remained, like this man, were forced to live in primitive conditions. He is drinking from a broken pipe because it is the best remaining source of water. (AC)

The Tokyo urban area (which included Yokohama) was hit by more bombs than any of Japan's other major cities. The comparative tonnage is shown here. Three-quarters of the bomb tonnage dropped on the Tokyo urban area were incendiaries. Only a quarter were the high explosives primarily used in precision bombing. (AC)

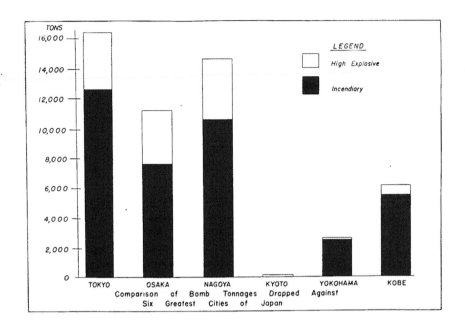

of B-29s dropped a mix of high-explosives and incendiaries on an urban area of Tokyo, had burned out 1 square mile of the city, a poor return given the size of the strike. Yet the subsequent fire raids burned massive chunks out of the city. The change was due less to the Japanese than a change in US tactics.

Active Japanese air defenses were most effective when the US bombers were at or below 28,000ft. When the B-29s flew between 28,000 to 33,000ft, both Japanese antiaircraft artillery and Japanese fighters were operating at their ceilings. The antiaircraft shells made it that high only when the guns were pointing almost straight up, which meant the B-29s had to fly almost directly over a gun position to have a chance of being hit. Japan lacked the gun density to pose a significant threat to high-flying B-29s. Japanese fighters flew sluggishly at 28,000 to 33,000ft. Only a skilled pilot could reach and successfully attack a B-29 at those altitudes.

Equally, the B-29s were almost totally ineffective at those altitudes, even when conditions were optimal for precision bombing. Often, clouds obscured the target. Even when the skies were clear, winds at those altitudes made accuracy impossible. The only successful precision strikes occurred when the B-29s attacked at lower altitudes, 18,000 to 27,000ft. At those altitudes, both antiaircraft and fighters of the density encountered over Tokyo were deadly unless they could be neutralized.

That could not be done without fighter escort and radar jamming, tools that were unavailable until April. Until then, flying low enough to ensure bombing accuracy during a daytime precision strike would result in unacceptable losses. Until something else was tried, the Twentieth Air Force would continue getting publicity without accomplishing a lot in bombing results.

Hansell was not the man to try something else. He was not just an apostle of air power. He was firmly a high church air power believer. His faith in daylight precision bombing was absolute. He had justifications for why it had not worked previously; too few aircraft with crews too inexperienced to bomb effectively. When pressed to use B-29s for mine missions, he demurred. When ordered to try a fire-bombing raid, he approached it half-heartedly.

An exasperated Arnold replaced him with Curtis LeMay. While LeMay was another air power true believer, he was willing to try anything once. He kept using any successful tactic as long as it provided results. After a proof-of-concept fire raid on February 25, he decided the tactic had merit, but needed changes to be truly effective. He concluded mass was the critical factor. He made the next fire raid a maximum effort with 330 B-29s.

He also more than doubled the bombload of the February 25 prototype mission, eliminating high-explosive bombs to carry more incendiaries. He did this by attacking at night, when antiaircraft and fighters were less effective, and attacking at very low altitudes. Unlike the earlier raid, the result overwhelmed Tokyo's fire prevention services. The Japanese were incapable of stopping the raids.

It set the mold for subsequent incendiary raids. Subsequent fire raids against Japan's largest cities, including five more on the Tokyo urban area, were all maximum effort raids, with 300 to 560 aircraft, and the heaviest possible load of incendiaries that could be carried. Yet LeMay was not locked into a single solution. When the May 26 fire raid against Tokyo, a night raid, resulted in unexpectedly high casualties, LeMay changed tactics. The next raid was conducted during the day, with the bombers attacking at high altitude to foil antiaircraft and a fighter escort to stave off Japanese fighters.

Under LeMay, the Twentieth Air Force adapted quickly to new opportunities. Once Iwo Jima became available as an emergency strip, damaged bombers or those low on gasoline had a place to land halfway to the Marianas. That allowed gasoline margins to be cut and bombloads increased. Similarly, once ECM and fighter escorts became available, B-29s made daylight raids at lower altitudes. This increased accuracy. Increasing air and ground crew experience also improved bombing accuracy and reduced mission aborts due to mechanical issues.

Could Japan have won the battle for Tokyo? If the US had not changed tactics, possibly. TF38 could not do enough damage by itself to reduce Tokyo. A lot of resources had been invested in the B-29; the return on those resources was negative through February 1945. The losses experienced through that month were acceptable, but only if Japan was suffering proportional damage. It was not, and a significant amount of fuel and munitions was being expended to no good purpose. The B-29 would have been invaluable for long-range reconnaissance, and even to provide tactical support of US Army and Navy actions. Theater commanders were pushing for reassignment of these aircraft.

By March, Arnold and LeMay were under increasing pressure to use B-29s to support theater and tactical operations. Even with the successful fire raids of March, LeMay had been

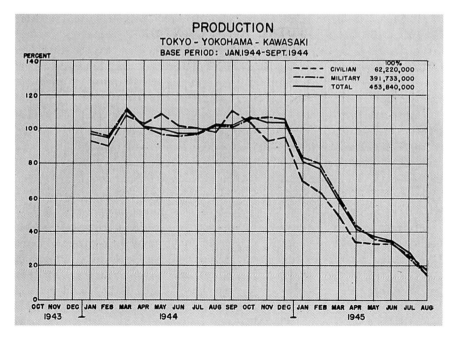

Production in the Tokyo urban area peaked in November 1944 and dropped thereafter. Even before the March fire raid, production had dropped by 40 percent. Losing access to raw materials outside Japan left factories idle. These shortages may have contributed more to Tokyo's production drops than bombing did. (AC)

forced to shelve strategic missions in order to bomb Kyushu airfields during April 1945. Had he gone through March sticking to high-altitude bombing and without that month's devastating fire raids, it is possible the strategic air offensive against Japan would have been abandoned. The B-29s would have been switched to theater operations. That would have given Japan victory at Tokyo. This book would be far different.

If Japan had invested more in antiaircraft artillery, radar, and night fighters, and improved tactics and operational doctrine (especially ground-controlled interception for fighters), the battle could have gone dramatically differently. They did not, and had no interest in developing a culture where individual warriors made themselves subservient to central planning. Japanese pilots were willing to ram B-29s, but unwilling to make coordinated attacks. They were bound to lose once the US developed effective offensive bombing tactics.

A more interesting question is whether bombing was the main cause of Tokyo's production losses. Tokyo reached its peak productivity between September and December 1944. Production dropped 40 percent between December 1944 and the end of February 1945, a period when strategic bombing was almost totally ineffective. That was a period when imports to Japan dropped precipitously, primarily due to US submarines attacking Japanese and the US carrier raid in the South China Sea severing Japanese supply lines from French Indochina, the Dutch East Indies, and Malaya and Burma. Operation *Starvation* hardened the blockade. After February 1945, Japan had to rely almost exclusively on domestic resources.

Against the argument that blockade was the primary reason Tokyo ground to a halt was the fact that production of industries relied on raw materials available domestically. Production of tools and machines, electrical equipment, and metals and metal products crashed only after the March fire raid. In some cases, the drop was as much as 70 percent. Production in the tools, electrical equipment, and machine parts sectors was highly dependent on home factories heavily hit during fire raids. While blockade helped bring down Japan, the destruction of Tokyo's industrial section was just as crucial. A starved-out Japan may have been less willing to surrender than a Japan starved out *and* bombed out.

Surviving aircraft

There are many surviving examples of aircraft types that fought over Tokyo during World War II. On the US side, there are 26 surviving examples of B-29s, 250 P-51s, 31 surviving F6F Hellcats, 60 F4Us, 79 Avengers, and nine Helldivers. No B-32s exist.

Fewer examples of Japanese aircraft survived. For the Imperial Navy, 30 A6M Zero (along with a few replicas) and four Kawanishi N1K1 *Shiden* and one J2M3 *Raiden* are still around. Five Ki-43 *Hayabusa* and five Ki-61 *Hien* exist. One example each of a Ki-84 *Hayate*, Kawasaki Ki-45 *Toryu*, and Nakajima J1N1 *Gekkō* exist.

Whether these aircraft actually fought over Tokyo is a different and more difficult question to answer. That at least one B-29 that did so still exists is absolutely certain. *Bockscar*, which dropped an atom bomb on Nagasaki, practiced for its atomic mission by dropping a conventionally armed replica of the "Fat Man" bomb on the ruins of the Musashino factory. Of the remaining 25 B-29s, eight are combat veteran, including two others belonging to the 509th Composite Group. Those two did not bomb Tokyo, although it is likely one of the remaining six did. Two B-29s are still flying, but neither left the United States during World War II.

It is likely that none of the surviving P-51s fought over Tokyo. Relatively few of the P-51s that fought on the sharp end in the Pacific in the last months of the war returned to the United States. The aircraft carriers used on Operation *Magic Carpet* (the repatriation of over 8 million American military personnel) carried personnel back to the States, not Army aircraft. After that, there was little incentive to repatriate P-51s on Iwo Jima. Most were used in the Far East until they were no longer needed and scrapped there. There were plenty of war-surplus Mustangs in the States in the postwar years.

Similarly, most of the aircraft that fought with the Fast Carrier Force in battles over and around Tokyo were discarded after the war. There were plenty of newly constructed Avengers, Hellcats, Corsairs, and Helldivers for the Navy's postwar demands. They were retained, not battle-weary veterans.

It is far more likely the surviving Japanese aircraft were veterans of this campaign, especially late-war examples. During the occupation, the United States sent teams into occupied Japan to study their war-making capabilities. They brought back samples of representative Japanese aircraft for analysis in the United States. This includes the *Shiden*, *Raiden*, *Toryu*, and *Gekkō*. As Tokyo was where technology teams harvested their samples, it is likely some of these aircraft fought over Tokyo.

None of the surviving *Hien* seem to have seen service in Home Defense units. The surviving *Hayate* was captured in the Philippines, so did not take part in defending the Home Islands. They did not participate.

Most surviving aircraft, Japanese and US, are in the United States. A few are in Japan. For those interested in seeing the most different types of aircraft which participated, Japanese and Allied, your best choice seems to be the Pima Air and Space Museum in Tucson, Arizona.

"Doc," one of two B-29s still capable of flight, doing a fly-by during the 2022 Wings Over Houston Airshow. Built in 1944, it was converted to a radar calibration aircraft and spent World War II and its entire Air Force career in the United States. The website for the organization operating it is https://www.b29doc. com/. (AC)

FURTHER READING

I could do worse than recommend readers to read my own *Japan 1944–45: LeMay's B-29 strategic bombing campaign* (Osprey Publishing, 2019). Although this book focused on a subset of *Japan 1944–45*, I ignored it in preparing this book, and started my research from a blank slate. I did that because I found new and better sources of information for the Tokyo campaign than I had back then.

This included the *Reports of the U.S. Naval Technical Mission to Japan, 1945–1946* (U.S. Naval History Division Washington, D.C. 1974) and a wealth of reports by the U.S. Strategic Bombing Survey. The former was a survey of Japanese naval technology conducted by the US Navy in the wake of Japan's defeat.

The latter is a set of 108 lengthy reports on different aspects of the air war in the Pacific. Many were focused on the Tokyo urban region. They went into significant detail about activities involving Tokyo, including reports on individual aircraft factories in and around the city. Their conclusions should be filtered through the preparers' desire to prove the decisiveness of air power. Their statistics are accurate and revealing. Most are now available online, significantly more than were available in 2018. (Books available online are marked with an "*" below.)

Principal sources used for this book were:

Craven, Wesley Frank and Cate, James Lea (editors), *The Army Air Forces in World War II, Volume Five: The Pacific: Matterhorn to Nagasaki, June 1944 to August 1945*, Office of Air Force History, Washington, D.C., 1983*

Hansell, Haywood S., *The Strategic Air War Against Germany and Japan: A Memoir*, Office of Air Force History, United States Air Force, Washington, D.C., 1986*

LeMay, Curtis E., *Combat Crew Manual, XX Bomber Command*, APO 493 Saipan, December 1944*

LeMay, Curtis E. and Yenne, Bill, *Superfortress: The Story of the B-29 and American Air Power*, Berkely Books, New York, NY 1989

Price, Alfred, *Instruments of Darkness: The History of Electronic Warfare, 1939–1945*, Frontline Books, Barnsley, South Yorkshire, 2017

United States Strategic Bombing Survey, *Effects of Incendiary Bomb Attacks on Japan: A Report on Eight Cities*, Washington, D.C., 1947

United States Strategic Bombing Survey, *Effects of Air Attacks on Urban Complex Tokyo-Kawasaki-Yokohama*, Washington, D.C., 1947*

United States Strategic Bombing Survey, *The Effects of Air Attack on Japanese Urban Economy*, Washington, D.C., 1947*

United States Strategic Bombing Survey, *Effects of Two Thousand, One Thousand, and Five Hundred Pound Bombs on Japanese Targets (a Report on Eight Incidents)*, Washington, D.C., 1947

United States Strategic Bombing Survey, *The Effects of Strategic Bombing on Japan's War Economy*, Washington, D.C., 1947*

United States Strategic Bombing Survey, *The Japanese Aircraft Industry*, Washington, D.C., 1947*

United States Strategic Bombing Survey, *Japanese Air Power*, Washington, D.C., 1946*

United States Strategic Bombing Survey, *Japanese Air Weapons and Tactics*, Washington, D.C., 1947*

United States Strategic Bombing Survey, *The Japanese Aircraft Industry*, Washington, D.C., 1947*

The Twentieth Air Force used M-66 2,000lb bombs against aircraft factories for the first time during the April 13 raid on the Musashi aircraft engine plant. Postwar target damage analysis shows how effectively they penetrated the sturdy reinforced-concrete main building. (AC)

INDEX

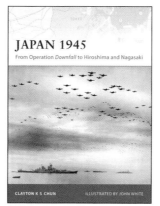
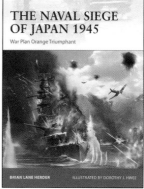

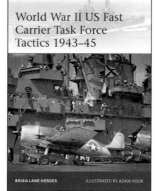
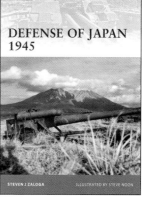

AIR CAMPAIGN

How history's greatest air wars were planned and fought, and why they were won and lost

In November 1944, the US Army Air Force launched a 111-plane B-29 strike against Tokyo, the first since the morale-boosting Doolittle Raid of 1942. From then until VJ-Day, Tokyo would be hit 25 times: in 20 raids from B-29s based in the Marianas and by five strikes from US Navy carrier task forces. The campaign included the single deadliest air raid in human history, when an estimated 100,000 people were killed by the firestorm created by Operation *Meetinghouse* on March 10, 1945.

This book, the first to examine the full history of the United States' air campaign against the greatest target in Japan, looks at the complex array of airpower that the USAAF and US Navy used to eliminate Tokyo's strategic value. It considers how the campaign developed from daylight bombing to firebombing and antiship mining, and finally how the target was handed over to the US Navy, whose carrier-based bombers and fighter-bombers battered Tokyo during July and August 1945.

Using superb battlescenes, maps, and 3D diagrams, this volume presents a detailed picture of how Tokyo was vanquished from the air.

INCLUDES:

- BATTLESCENES
- BIRD'S-EYE VIEWS
- MAPS AND DIAGRAMS
- EXPERT ANALYSIS

www.ospreypublishing.com

OSPREY PUBLISHING
ISBN 978-1-4728-6035-4

FSC

9 781472 860354
52500

www.ospreypublishing.com

UK £16.99 | US $25.00 | CAN $33.00

AFGHANISTAN
1979–88

Soviet air power against the *mujahideen*

MARK GALEOTTI | ILLUSTRATED BY EDOUARD A. GROULT

Author

Dr Mark Galeotti is a globally recognised expert on Russian politics and security, who has taught in the UK, US, Russia and Czech Republic, and written numerous books, including a number of Osprey titles, notably *Putin's Wars* (2022). He is based in the UK, where he runs the consultancy Mayak Intelligence, and is also an honorary professor at UCL School of Slavonic and East European Studies and a senior associate fellow with both RUSI and the Council on Geostrategy. Educated at Cambridge University and the LSE, he has been attached to the Foreign Office, advised NATO and several governments, and wrote his PhD on the Soviet war in Afghanistan.

Illustrator

Edouard A. Groult grew up inspired by watching historical documentaries with his father and developed a fascination for historical and fantasy art. Following art studies in both Paris and Belgium, he worked as a concept artist in the videogame industry and, in recent years, he has also undertaken historical commissions for magazines. He lives and works in Oxford.

Other titles in the series

ROLLING THUNDER 1965–68
Johnson's air war over Vietnam

RICHARD P. HALLION | ILLUSTRATED BY ADAM TOOBY

ACM No: 3 • **ISBN:** 9781472823205

OPERATION *LINEBACKER II* 1972
The B-52s are sent to Hanoi

MARSHALL L. MICHEL III | ILLUSTRATED BY JIM LAURIER

ACM No: 6 • **ISBN:** 9781472827609

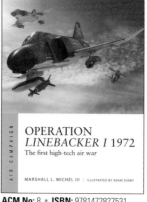

OPERATION *LINEBACKER I* 1972
The first high-tech air war

MARSHALL L. MICHEL III | ILLUSTRATED BY ADAM TOOBY

ACM No: 8 • **ISBN:** 9781472827531

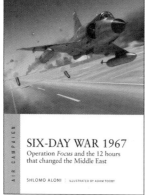

SIX-DAY WAR 1967
Operation *Focus* and the 12 hours that changed the Middle East

SHLOMO ALONI | ILLUSTRATED BY ADAM TOOBY

ACM No: 10 • **ISBN:** 9781472835277

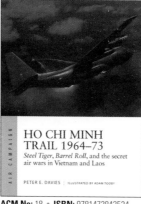

HO CHI MINH TRAIL 1964–73
Steel Tiger, *Barrel Roll*, and the secret air wars in Vietnam and Laos

PETER E. DAVIES | ILLUSTRATED BY ADAM TOOBY

ACM No: 18 • **ISBN:** 9781472842534

DESERT STORM 1991
The most shattering air campaign in history

RICHARD P. HALLION | ILLUSTRATED BY ADAM TOOBY

ACM No: 25 • **ISBN:** 9781472846969